WINDSCAPE

WINDSCAPE

Sam Wilding

www.stridentpublishing.co.uk

Published by
Strident Publishing Ltd
22 Strathwhillan Drive
The Orchard
Hairmyres
East Kilbride
G75 8GT

Tel: +44 (0)1355 220588
info@stridentpublishing.co.uk
www.stridentpublishing.co.uk

Published by Strident Publishing Limited, 2012
Text © Sam Wilding, 2012
Cover art by The Earlybird | Cover design by LawrenceMann.co.uk

ISBN 978-1-905537-92-1

Typeset in DIN by oscarkills

The publisher acknowledges support from Creative Scotland towards the publication of this title.

the publisher acknowledges investment from
Creative Scotland toward the publication of this book

BORN IN Helensburgh, Scotland, Sam Wilding grew up beside Loch Lomond on the very edge of the Scottish Highlands. He gained an honours degree in Zoology at Glasgow University and always maintained a strong interest in nature and the outdoors. His first novel, "The Magic Scales – Book One of the *Denthan* series" was published in 2008. He has written a further two novels in this series and is working on a set of ten picture books for younger children. *Windscape* is his fourth children's novel. Sam still writes and works near Loch Lomond, Scotland.

www.sam-wilding.com

This book is dedicated to the children of the Western Isles of Scotland, who are privileged to live in one of the most beautiful parts of the world.

My thanks and appreciation go out to Billy Scobie and Gregor Addison, for their encouragement; to the Western Isles Libraries, for their fantastic help and support during this project; and to my youngest daughter, Ruth, who listened to the story unfold every night, chapter by chapter.

I know, Ruth... it should have been called,
'Big Grey Spiny Things'.

CHAPTER ONE
HUSHWISH BAY

Jenny felt her father's rough hand fold around hers. Perched against the Needlestone above the bay, they were just out of the worst of the wind and cold. The heather shuddered at their feet and the stunted trees marking the edge of their land arched back from the sea. Cast by the strong gales into an array of gnarled and twisted limbs, the trees resembled a row of cowering old men. Harried by the western winds and battered by an angry sea, Hushwish Bay was still the most beautiful place Jenny had ever known.

"Can you see the markers, Jenny?" asked her father. "Can you see where they are going to build them?"

Her eyes half open, Jenny peered down over the heather until she saw the field beyond their farmhouse. Along its length, in the marshy dip before the dunes, six stone cairns shone like beacons in the morning sun. Jenny's stomach churned. "You're not going to let them go ahead, are you? Mum would have said no to all this, you know she would have."

"Your mother..." her father paused, squeezing her hand a little tighter, "...your mother would have wanted what was best for you, Jenny."

"And you think that *this* is what's best for me? How can you think that *this* is what's best for the farm, Dad?" said Jenny.

Unexpectedly, her father's face brightened. "Do you realise, Jenny, that they'll be over one hundred feet high? They'll be the tallest in the whole of the Hebrides."

"Whoopee-bloomin'-doo," Jenny murmured.

Although her father was suddenly talking like some eccentric scientist explaining the most wonderful invention ever, Jenny knew that he didn't want those things on the farm either.

As their old sheepdog, Lord, began barking down in the steading, she thought about her father getting up during the middle of the night. He'd taken to clattering about, making tea and pacing around at the strangest of times. She knew that he was worried about the bank, and what they'd said. She knew he was worried about something called repossession. The letter from the bank in Glasgow had given her father until the end of the month. He had until then to raise the amount needed to cover his debts. Jenny knew that there were only two days left before the month was up.

"But Dad," said Jenny, "the bay won't be the same. Our home won't be the same. I've heard all about those things and what they do. They're horrible. Up at the Petries' farm, they cut the birds from the air with their horrible arms. They whistle like giant swans in the daytime and howl like phantoms in the dead of night."

"Nonsense. Who told you that rubbish?" said her father.

"Pavel," said Jenny, suddenly feeling a bit stupid.

"Ha! I might have known." He cuddled her in closer until she could smell the tobacco from his damp, tweed coat. "It won't be that bad, Jenny," he assured her. "Look, we'll only have six of them. They'll sit between that fank where the tups are now and the cliff." His fingers fluttered between the small field where they kept the rams and a rocky outcrop littered with frantic fulmars and cackling kittiwakes.

"But, Dad..." she protested.

"That's the end of it, Jenny." He closed his deep-set eyes and, after a long sigh, whispered, "I've no choice."

Jenny didn't want to get angry with him but she couldn't help herself. "So, you've said yes to the men who came to the farm last week? Has Murdoch bullied you into it?"

Her father didn't answer.

Jenny felt a wave of frustration rise inside her. "So you haven't said yes? So you didn't sign the form?"

Her father's brow, rutted like a newly ploughed field, suddenly deepened. Something had caught his attention. She felt his big, calloused hand slip from hers.

"Who's that on the beach?" he said. He rummaged for the binoculars in his thick tweed coat. "I can never find the bloomin' things...always in a different pocket than you think... hopeless..." He patted each pocket of his coat in turn.

The beach, a lick of pure white sand that edged the turquoise water in the bay, was usually deserted, but not today. A solitary figure walked along the tide line for about a hundred yards and then stopped.

"It's just a tourist," said Jenny. "Look, he's picking up some driftwood."

Her father grunted. "We need that wood."

"He probably doesn't know that it's our beach, Dad," said Jenny, her frustration changing into concern.

Her father stood up, the ancient Needlestone monolith looming over him. "Well, he's going to find out that it's our beach, and our wood, pretty sharpish." He began to walk down through the heather.

The wind whipped Jenny's blonde hair into her face as she tried to keep up with him. She had to pull the long strands from her eyes every few steps. Below them, on the beach, a further three figures had joined the first. She caught her father's sleeve. "They've got stuff with them. What are they carrying, Dad?"

Her father tugged free of her grip and quickened his pace.

"There's a woman with a pram," shouted Jenny, skidding down behind him.

On the beach, the woman dragged the pram across the dark line of seaweed and debris, its wheels useless in the deep sand.

Jenny could tell her father was getting angrier by the second. As they neared the farmhouse he cursed and whistled on Lord.

The old dog replied with a deep bark.

Lord was just as bad tempered as her father, and they would be a force to be reckoned with if the people on the beach were up to no good.

Another six figures suddenly joined the first four.

Where are they all coming from? she thought. She didn't recognise any of them, and she could see now that they were carrying cardboard boxes and something long and white that she couldn't quite make out. *Is it a flagpole?*

A blue minibus had been parked up behind the lambing shed. A second bus was coming down the lane. "Dad, be careful!" she yelled.

Her father was running and Lord was snapping at his heels, barking and yelping like a pup.

Her heart thumping, Jenny knew something was very wrong. These people didn't seem friendly.

A further dozen or so strangers poured out of the second minibus. They were carrying more wood and more boxes. One man, with a scraggy beard, struggled with a five-gallon fuel can.

Fifty yards from the dunes, her father began shouting at the strangers, but they ignored him. He soon reached the top of the ridge, his big heavy coat flapping in the wind, Lord barking at his side, but still they ignored him.

She'd have to run faster to catch him up. She'd seen the strangers building something, digging something into place, but now the dunes were blocking her view.

The fine sand spilled into her shoes as she climbed up the face of the nearest dune, handfuls of marram grass sliding through her fingers as she pulled herself higher. "Dad," she panted, "wait on me."

As the salty breeze cut into her at the top of the dune, she froze. She could see what they'd been building...

CHAPTER TWO
THE PYRE

Is it a cross? No, it's a *windmill*, thought Jenny, a dummy, mock-up version of one of the big white turbines that would be built on their farm. Two rough-looking men were digging it into the wet sand. The rest of the mob piled wood and cardboard boxes around the white pole that formed the main support. Three white, wicker paddles jutted out at awkward angles to form the blades.

Jenny felt her heart thumping against her chest.

The whole scene looked unreal, like some weird dream. *Why would they build that thing on their beach?*

Her father was running full pelt across the sand, Lord stupidly snapping at his heels instead of barking at the strangers.

"Stop there, Hamish!" shouted the man with the scraggy beard.

Jenny realised that it was Mr Belfield, the church factor. She hadn't recognised him at first, with his new beard.

Jenny skittered down over the last few yards of dune before thudding into a rigid tuft of grass at its base. "Uh!"

Winded, she knelt up and dusted herself down.

She heard Mr Belfield yell at her father again, "Hamish, I'm warning you, keep back."

Undeterred, her father sprinted through the mob and leapt on top of Belfield, yanking him down onto the wet sand by the hood of his coat.

Fuel spilled from the open canister as it toppled onto the sand.

Jenny watched her father step away from Belfield. He turned to face the rest of the crowd.

They circled him like a pack of hungry animals. As her father picked up Belfield's shovel, two of the bigger men moved forward.

Lord growled and snapped at them.

"Leave him alone," screamed Jenny, but the crashing waves and harsh wind smothered her thin voice.

The woman with the pram spotted her first. She tugged on the sleeve of a big man standing next to her and pointed at Jenny. They began to walk towards her but soon stopped when her father swung the shovel in warning.

"Just hold it there, missus." Her father stabbed the shovel into the wet sand and pointed up the beach to the minibuses. "Now, take your toys with you and get off of my beach." Her father's face was redder than Jenny had ever seen it.

"We just want to make a peaceful protest," said the woman with the pram.

Her father rounded on her.

"Trying to set my beach on fire is hardly a peaceful protest, missus." He stabbed a finger at the fuel can.

A burly man lunged forward and pulled the shovel out of the sand, but her father grabbed the top of the handle and held on tight.

A skinny man with a stick jumped on her father's back and he began to lose his balance.

Jenny ran forward. She picked up a floppy piece of kelp and lashed out at the skinny man's back.

Lord sank his teeth into the burly man's leg. He screamed and dropped the spade. Hands grabbed her and pulled her back. She tried to scream but the woman covered her mouth. The smell of cigarettes from her long fingers made Jenny gag as they pressed against her lips. She heard her father roar in anger. He was fighting the men who held him. Lord was barking and snarling. There was a loud bang and Jenny felt a flash of heat on her face. She fell to the ground. "Dad!" she yelled again.

Through the tangle of legs and arms Jenny saw the woven shape of the windmill ignite. The sea breeze strengthened and black, acrid smoke soon wafted up towards them. Jenny began to cough.

A man caught hold of her and dragged her back from the flames.

"Let her go, Belfield!" Her father's voice sounded strange.

Jenny couldn't stop coughing.

Her father broke free of the group who were holding him and pushed Belfield and the woman to the ground. He pulled Jenny away from the strangers.

Belfield spun round and stood up to face them.

"Hamish..."

"You should know better, Belfield," gasped her father. "These people you've brought onto my land don't even live here."

"You're the last one," said Belfield. "If you cave in to

Murdoch, give them consent to build, then the whole coastline will be ruined."

"We've had enough!" shrieked the woman.

Thin and wiry with tangled grey hair, she looked like one of the witches from Macbeth. Her voice was very posh but it dripped with resentment. "This is what we'll do to your turbines if you put them here!" She pointed to the wicker windmill. It crackled and sparked in the background.

Her father's hands were dripping with sweat. "Get off my land," he panted.

"We'll go," said Belfield. "And, for the record, it didn't have to be like this."

"Like what?" said her father, his big frame silhouetted by the blazing arms of the windmill. Flecks of black ash, caught in the wind, spiralled up into the darkening sky behind him. "You've played this all wrong, Belfield. I didn't really have much of a choice but you and your cronies have just made up my mind."

The woman's face softened. "You can't spoil this place, you..."

"I can do whatever I want to, missus. And I'll tell you this: if I have to stand guard here every day to make sure you keep off my land, I will. You are a crazy, deluded bunch of thugs who have no respect for my land or..." he paused, his brow dripping with moisture, "...my daughter and-"

Her father stopped mid sentence and clutched his chest. His lips still struggled to find the words but his face was a picture of pain.

"Dad!" Jenny gasped.

Slowly, her father crumpled onto his knees and dropped the shovel.

He groaned and slumped forward.

As the people edged back, Jenny ran forwards.

Lord was already licking her father's face. "Someone..." Jenny felt dizzy. "Someone go and get help!"

A man with long hair produced a mobile and dialled. He held it up to the sky and then stared maniacally at the screen. "There's no signal."

Belfield rushed over to Jenny. He took her father's hand. "Hamish?"

Jenny began to cry. "Look at what you've done."

She pushed Belfield away from her father. "Get back!"

The strangers were beginning to melt away. Her eyes were blurred. She heard a minibus start up. She cupped her father's head in her lap. "Dad, they're going to get help."

Belfield hovered at the tide line. He stood amongst a tangle of seaweed and crab claws. The remains of a seagull's wing fluttered against his big boots. "What you are doing is against God's will, Hamish MacLeod."

"Shut up!" yelled Jenny. She felt her strength begin to ebb away. Her father's eyes were closing. "Shut up and get help before it's too late!"

Belfield wavered for a long moment and then set off in the direction of the minibuses.

Jenny mopped her father's brow with her golden hair. He was cold, his eyes closed tight. "Dad," she whispered. Her body shook and her tears dripped onto her father's cheek.

A few feet away, the pyre crackled. She could feel its heat on her wet face.

Hushwish Bay was empty.

Jenny was alone with Lord and her father, the burning windmill slowly disintegrating behind her.

Oblivious, the lumbering white gannets continued to glide and then dive into the blue water of the bay. Only Lord seemed to share her grief. He nuzzled into her father's big tweed coat and whined.

CHAPTER THREE
THE MURDOCHS

After the ambulance, the doctors and do-gooders had left the farm, Jenny sat in her mother's big flowery chair and stared out over the bay. The old chair, covered in swirling yellow and red roses, was still a magical place for Jenny. She could feel her mother's presence there, still trace the slightest hint of her perfume. The sweet familiar scent made Jenny feel that her mother could call her through for dinner at any moment. But she never would, and now her father was on his way to Glasgow. A heart attack, the doctor had said. A cardio-something or other...

"Jenny, do you want to come with us now?" asked Mrs Murdoch, a large buxom lady with a permanent frown on her face.

"I suppose," said Jenny.

"Mr Murdoch and Pavel will help you with your stuff."

"Why couldn't I go with my dad?" asked Jenny.

Mrs Murdoch increased the intensity of her frown by several notches, screwing up her face until it resembled a forlorn, pouting pumpkin. "Now, now, Jenny. You heard what the doctor said. He told you that your father needed to rest.

You don't want him worrying about where you're going to stay in Glasgow, or what you're going to eat. Your father knows you're safe here."

Jenny knew that she wouldn't be allowed to remain in the farmhouse by herself. "I'll get my things," she said.

Pavel, who at thirteen was just a little older than Jenny, smiled and placed a green duffel bag on the rug at her feet. "I put toothpaste and clothes and a few books in for you," he said. "I know you like books."

Still not completely tuned into Pavel's accent, Jenny nodded politely and began to poke around the contents of the bag. "My purse," she said. "I'll just get my purse."

"You won't be needing your purse, Jenny," said Mrs Murdoch. "You'll be our guest at Hilltop Farm until your father returns."

"I'll take it, just the same," said Jenny. "It has my keepsakes and stuff."

"We'd better get a move on," said Mr Murdoch. A well-dressed man, with a prominent nose and rounded belly, he'd just walked in from outside. The light was fading and rain had begun to patter on the living room window. "I want to check on the cattle before it's dark," he said. "Pavel, get Jenny's bag into the jeep and make room for Lord in the trailer."

"Yes, Mr Murdoch," said Pavel. He winked at Jenny and lifted the duffel bag over his broad shoulders.

Jenny found her purse on the mantelpiece and secretly slipped the spare key from under the marble clock into her pocket. She wanted a way back into her own house if necessary.

"Sandy had hoped to be here too," said Mrs Murdoch, "but he's still at his friend's house in Stornoway."

Jenny was pleased Sandy wasn't there. He was the school

bully, although she bet Mrs Murdoch would never believe it. Spoiled rotten and rarely questioned, even by the teachers, Sandy Murdoch was a nasty piece of work. "That's a shame," she said, trying her best to be polite.

"Yes, Sandy wanted to help," said Mrs Murdoch. "He said so on the phone."

Pavel fixed Jenny a look as he attached an old lead to Lord's collar. The look said, quite plainly – *'Yeh right. Sure he did'.*

Jenny knew that Sandy Murdoch bullied Pavel too. As they walked to the Murdoch's jeep, Jenny stared at Pavel. He was a funny one. Tall and lanky, with an old man's stoop, Pavel had lived and worked on the Murdoch's farm ever since his dad had taken on the role of head shepherd. Jenny knew he was Polish but everyone had thought he was Russian when he came to their school at first. They'd all heard actors doing Russian accents in James Bond films, and had decided that that's what Pavel sounded like: a Bond baddie. Some of the smart-alec numpties, like Sandy Murdoch, had called him a Ruskie and worse, but the teachers came down hard on name-calling at Carthern School, and for once Sandy Murdoch was no exception.

Yet, Pavel was more than capable of taking care of himself. He explained to those who wanted to listen that he was not a Ruskie, as they put it. The Russians and the Polish people had quite a chequered history, according to Pavel.

Mr Murdoch turned the key in the ignition and pulled away from Hushwish Farm.

Jenny spun round in her seat to look out the back window as they bumped along the rocky lane. Hushwish Farm looked isolated and dark. The colour had gone from the sky.

Mr Murdoch, the man sitting only inches away from her,

was the main driving force behind the wind farm project. Everyone knew that he'd done some kind of deal. She still didn't believe that her father would have given in. As they went over the brow of the hill, she glimpsed one of the stone cairns and then turned back round to face the front. Her dad was sure to sign the contract now. The protestors had ruined the whole thing. Her dad would build the windmills, now that they'd riled him.

"Are you okay, Jenny?" enquired Mrs Murdoch.

"Fine," said Jenny, snapping out of her thoughts, but she wasn't fine. She was worried sick about her dad.

As if reading her mind, Pavel cleared his throat. "The doctor said you could phone the hospital later on tonight."

"He did?" She twisted round to face Mrs Murdoch. "Is that okay?"

"Of course it is, Jenny," said Mrs Murdoch, her eyes fixing on Pavel.

In turn, Mr Murdoch gave Mrs Murdoch a stern look in the rear view mirror.

Maybe I shouldn't have asked, thought Jenny.

CHAPTER FOUR
THE LETTER

Hilltop Farm was totally alien to Jenny. It was a world of fitted kitchens, flat-screen TVs and flickering laptops. Although Hilltop was only two miles away from Hushwish, it stood resplendent amongst the heather and rocks of Harris. Newly built, the Murdochs' farm seemed out of place to many of the families round about. To Jenny's father, it represented the end of the old traditions on the Island, but it had also offered him a lifeline.

"You're thinking about your father?" said Pavel.

She placed her green duffel bag on the bed and stared up at Pavel's kind face. "I'm thinking about the wind farm and those idiots who caused him to..."

"There, there, Jenny." Awkwardly, Pavel patted her back and sat on the bed beside her. "They only wanted to object."

"Object?" Jenny felt her stomach knot with rage.

Pavel stumbled over his words, "They went about it badly. They made a muck of..."

"They were completely out of order!" Jenny hissed.

"Yes, they were," Pavel conceded.

"Everything was much clearer before the windmills

started sprouting up everywhere," said Jenny.

"Mr Murdoch says some of the protestors have been arrested," said Pavel. "The police will probably want a statement from you."

"They will?" said Jenny. Sheepishly, she stared at her feet. "I'm sorry for biting your head off, Pavel."

"It's okay. You've had a terrible day." Pavel gave her a big toothy smile. It faded, however, as his mind seemed to drift elsewhere. "Sandy will be back soon."

"Brilliant," said Jenny.

"You know, I kind of agree with the protestors, in a way," said Pavel.

Jenny bristled.

"Not in the way they did it," he added quickly. "No, that was wrong but..."

"But what?" asked Jenny.

"But I'm not sure that a whole bank of hundred-foot high windmills is the answer."

"Oh, Pavel, I don't like the idea of them either, but what happened today has made me think," said Jenny.

"You know it was Murdoch who started the whole wind farm thing here, don't you?" said Pavel.

"Dad said it was," said Jenny.

"He's persuaded six farms to sign up already, but the agency he deals with needs enough turbines to justify the investment. They needed a seventh farm, your farm. The protestors knew that."

"So dad's not given Murdoch the go-ahead?"

"I don't think so," said Pavel. "I don't think the protestors were 'crying over spilt milk', as you put it. I think their protest was a last ditch attempt to stop the whole wind farm project."

"My dad says that we need the money from the wind farm to keep our farm. We have to pay off the bank or..."

"But you'll change everything. That's like cutting your throat to spite your face."

"Your nose... cutting off your nose," Jenny corrected, absentmindedly. She sighed and stood up to look out of the window. Her head hurt as she tried to get everything straight. She sighed as a black pick-up drew into the newly chipped driveway.

"Sandy's back," said Jenny.

"Look, Jenny. Before Sandy begins his nonsense, I want to show you something."

"What?" said Jenny, suddenly confused.

"Did you know that Mr Murdoch gets all your mail?"

"Yes. It saves the postie coming all the way along the headland."

The gravel churned as the pick-up drew out of the yard.

"So how do you know you're getting every single letter?" asked Pavel. He took her hand and led her down the wooden steps to the ground floor.

"What are you saying, Pavel?" she whispered. "Where are we going?"

"Quick, before Sandy gets inside. Mrs Murdoch's busy in the kitchen and Mr Murdoch's out checking his precious cattle," Pavel whispered back.

"Where are you taking me?" Jenny pressed.

"I've seen Mr Murdoch in the kitchen with your letters," said Pavel.

"In the kitchen?"

"Yes."

As they edged past the kitchen door, the security lights

blasted on outside.

"I've seen him steam your letters open with the kettle," continued Pavel.

"Why would he do that?" asked Jenny.

"I don't know but I've watched him doing it," he said again.

"Pavel, someone's coming," said Jenny.

Sandy Murdoch was crunching up the gravel path outside the front door.

"Shhh! He'll go up to his room first," said Pavel. "He always does. Quick! Follow me!" Pavel ducked under the glass window set into the front door.

Jenny copied him. Still confused by the whole episode, she followed him into the Murdochs' posh living room.

"Right," said Pavel. "We've got about two minutes."

"Why didn't we do this earlier?" she whispered.

"Mrs Murdoch would have been creeping about. This is the one moment, our window of opportunity, Jenny."

Pavel always quoted little sayings like this, she remembered. It was annoying enough at the best of times, but right at that moment Jenny's head was spinning and she felt like telling him to shut up. "We get all of our letters the next day. You give them to me in school, during the week."

"You've not been getting all the letters," said Pavel.

"How do you know?" said Jenny, becoming angry again.

"Because, after I saw him do his thing with the kettle, I checked. I counted how many letters were addressed to your farm and then how many he actually gave you. Last Tuesday three arrived with your address on them, but he only gave me two to pass on."

Jenny scrunched up her face. "What are you talking about?"

"He puts the letters he keeps back from you in here." Pavel

slid open a small wooden drawer set into the piano stool.

"He's got a secret drawer in a piano stool?"

"Sneaky, eh?" said Pavel.

Outside in the hall, the front door clicked open.

They both froze, the secret drawer half open. Pavel reached down and lifted out a small bundle of letters. "Here. They're all yours."

Jenny fumbled with the letters; she looked around anxiously, trying to think of some excuse for standing in the middle of the Murdochs' living room.

Pavel pressed his forefinger to his lips, widened his grey eyes and shook his head.

The unmistakable voice of Sandy Murdoch echoed out from the hallway. "What's for dinner, Mum?"

Muffled and someway off, Mrs Murdoch answered, "shepherd's pie and Brussels sprouts."

"Mingin'," shouted Sandy.

"What was that?" his mum asked.

"Humdingin'," muttered Sandy, with a chuckle. "Daft old bat."

Jenny could hear him hanging up his wet coat on the peg in the hall, muttering insults and cursing. Soon, he was clattering up the stairs.

"That's the letter, there," whispered Pavel.

The security lights from outside illuminated the living room.

Jenny tapped the letter at the top of the pile. "Is this the letter he hid from us last Tuesday?" asked Jenny.

Pavel nodded excitedly.

She peeled the top letter away from the bundle and studied the brown manila envelope. It had an official look to it. She could see where the glue had come away from the seal on the back. On the top left-hand corner she noticed a mark or stamp of some kind. She held it up to the window and read it out –"'Munro and Morrison Insurance'."

Pavel gripped her arm, but it was too late. With a whoosh and a loud creak, the living room door swung open and light flooded the room.

CHAPTER FIVE
THE PIANIST

Mrs Murdoch walked into the living room and stopped dead. "Pavel? Jenny? What are you doing in here?"

Pavel moved in front of Jenny and made little flicking movements with his hands behind his back. "Just showing Jenny your brilliant piano, Mrs Murdoch. I know she plays a little."

Behind Pavel, Jenny stuffed the official-looking letter down the belt of her jeans and shoved the rest of the bundle back into the piano stool.

"I'm not sure that I'm too happy about this, Pavel. I mean... I'm just about to serve dinner. Aren't you going back to your own house to be with your father?" said Mrs Murdoch. Her face was the colour of pickled beetroot.

"Yes, yes... my father should be back by now. He was up on the hill putting mineral tubs down for the lambs."

Mrs Murdoch's tone lightened a little as she turned to face Jenny. "So you play, Jenny?"

"A little," said Jenny, knowing fine-well she didn't play a note. She edged away from the piano.

"Sandy!" yelled Mrs Murdoch. She stuck her head back into

the hall. "Sandy, come down and hear Jenny play the piano."

Jenny's heart sank. She caught Pavel by the arm and dug in her nails.

Pavel pulled away. "Eh, well... must be getting back. I've already heard her anyway." He cupped his mouth and whispered to Mrs Murdoch in a furtive tone, "She's brilliant, by the way."

Jenny wanted to kick him, but he'd moved away too quickly.

Sandy Murdoch appeared beside his mother.

"Well, well... if it isn't Jenny MacLeod." He caught Pavel by the cuff of his coat as he squeezed past, and in a voice laced with venom hissed, *What are you doing in our house?"*

"Sandy," gasped Mrs Murdoch, as if witnessing a nasty, one-off event, "Pavel was helping Jenny with her things."

"More like, helping himself to her things," he muttered.

Ignoring the jibe, Pavel produced one of his toothy smiles and said goodnight.

The front door slammed, leaving Jenny, in more ways than one, to face the music. She took a deep breath and forced an expression of delight. "Is that shepherd's pie I can smell?"

Mrs Murdoch beamed. "It is indeed."

"It smells wonderful. Can we have some now?"

"Well, yes. But..."

"But we want to hear you play something first," said Sandy. "You've kept that one quiet, Jenny." He strolled into the room. "Imagine, mum, a talent like that in our midst and no one in the whole school knew a thing about it." He moved closer and eyed the piano stool. "Let's see. What have we here?"

Jenny flushed in terror. She could feel the sweat running down her back.

"Bach, Chopin... nah," said Sandy. He lifted the lid of the

piano seat and rummaged about. "What about a good old Scottish lament?"

Jenny could see that the 'secret drawer' had been left slightly open. The bundle of letters had stopped it from shutting properly.

Sandy was only inches above it, pulling out sheets of music.

"Look," said Jenny. "I am very hungry and totally drained."

"Oh, but you let Pavel hear you play," said Sandy, in a kind of pouting, pleading baby voice that made Jenny want to smash his face in.

"That was before I began to feel sick," blurted Jenny.

"You feel sick?" enquired Mrs Murdoch.

"I always get squeamish when I've not eaten for a while. A lack of sugar, according to Dr. Miller."

"A lack of confidence," said Sandy, unfolding the music to Highland Cathedral. He moved closer and whispered, *"or is it a lack of truth?"*

"What?" she gasped. She decided to go on the offensive. "If you're going to bully me here as well as at school, I'm going straight back to my own house."

There was a long silence only broken by the sound of the front door clicking open and a pair of boots being thrown under the stairs.

"That will be Mr Murdoch," said Mrs Murdoch. She eyed Sandy suspiciously. "We can listen to Jenny after dinner."

"Can't wait," beamed Sandy.

Mr Murdoch popped his head through the doorway. "Everyone all right?"

Jenny pulled down the edge of her jumper to cover the bulge of the letter in her belt and smiled. "Yes. Just getting hungry. I need to go upstairs and freshen up."

CHAPTER SIX
THE DISCUSSION

At the kitchen table the conversation soon turned to the subject of the protestors.

"What a bunch of absolute nutters," said Mr Murdoch.

Jenny studied his face trying to get the measure of the man who had hidden their letters. *Why had he kept back so many? What was in the letter she'd bundled into her duffel bag upstairs? What would an insurance company want with her father?*

"Jenny?" he prompted.

"Yes?" She stared blankly at Mr Murdoch for a few moments before nodding her head. "I think they are very sad people too," she said.

"Dangerous people, you mean," added Sandy. "They think they know what's best for this island and they don't even come from here."

"Apart from Belfield," added Mrs Murdoch, "and I thought he was a decent man."

"You never can tell these days," said Mr Murdoch. "Deluded and in deep with all sorts of demonstrators and sects according to Constable MacGregor."

Sandy became more animated as he shovelled the mince

and crusty potato into his big mouth. "I mean, windmills are good for the environment. They'll soon produce more than twenty per cent of our energy up here. They've got to be better than nuclear power or coal or oil or any of that stuff."

Although Sandy was a nasty bully, he wasn't daft. Jenny wondered who'd planted all those facts into his warped brain. "Why do you say that?" said Jenny.

"What do you think?" said Sandy.

"Well," said Jenny. "I think they ruin the place." Jenny was relieved that the conversation was steering away from her prowess on the piano.

Mr Murdoch stopped munching. "Ruin the place?"

"They churn up the peat bogs and..."

"Peat bogs," replied Sandy. "You've been listening to Pavel too much. I suppose he told you that the windmills act like big food blenders, mincing up all the birds that fly past."

"Not...in so many words," said Jenny. She suddenly felt a bit stupid.

"See!" shrieked Sandy. "I told you Pavel's bad news, Dad."

His dad wiped the gravy from his knife on the edge of his plate and said, "Pavel isn't a bad lad, Sandy. His head's just up in the clouds from time to time."

Sandy guffawed. "He's a..."

Mr Murdoch thumped the table. "His father is a very good shepherd, so don't go causing any more problems with your name-calling. Got it?"

There was a long, drawn-out silence at the table. All Jenny could hear was the clink of dishes and the rattle of cutlery.

Jenny liked this. The Murdochs fighting amongst themselves kept their thoughts away from her piano playing. She decided to break the silence and keep the conversation going in this direction for a bit longer. "It's not just Pavel who questions the wind farms you know."

"Really?" said Mr Murdoch.

"Mrs Harper, in school, says that the peat bogs are like Scotland's lungs," said Jenny.

"Like what?" laughed Mrs Murdoch, spraying the table top with a mixture of spit, potato and tomato sauce.

"Like Scotland's lungs," pressed Jenny. "You see, we don't have a rain forest or anything but we do have peat bogs. Seventeen percent of the whole world's blanket bog is here in Scotland. Pumping out oxygen. Helping us all breathe."

"Blanket bog?" said Mr Murdoch. "Why, you'd think you were one of those protestors yourself, Jenny, the way you're spouting nonsense like that."

"I like to learn that kind of stuff at school. I like to hear all sides to a story."

"I'll have to have a word with the school. A teacher filling children's heads with stuff and nonsense like that," said Mr Murdoch.

"*So,*" said Sandy, pointedly, "*you'd* rather have our skies full of black smoke, or our beaches littered with radioactive waste?"

Jenny was used to this tone. It was Sandy Murdoch's big bully tone. The one he used to threaten the younger kids like her.

This time it was Sandy who thumped his first down on the table. "It's only a few windmills. The sheep can still graze round about them. I don't understand why you're defending the nutters that caused your dad to..."

"*Sandy,*" warned Mrs Murdoch.

Jenny wondered why Mr Murdoch didn't tell Sandy off for

being rude, too. If she'd talked to anyone like that in her house, in front of her father, he would have grounded her for a week. She felt the anger inside her begin to boil again. "It's not just the windmills themselves; it's the roads and the concrete and the pylons and all the other stuff that goes along with them..." she caught her breath, "besides, I don't even care about all that. I don't want my beautiful beach, or any part of our farm spoiled by those things."

Mr Murdoch slowly shook his head. "There are a lot of people depending on them. There are a lot of people round here suffering real hardship."

Still boiling, Jenny answered, "I don't see any signs of hardship here."

Sitting in the gleaming new kitchen with the best of everything at their fingertips, Jenny guessed it was probably going to be a bit awkward for the Murdochs to come back at her now.

"We are better off than most," admitted Mr Murdoch, "though only through hard work and careful investment."

Yeah, thought Jenny. You're going to make another fortune from this wind farm too, aren't you?

Mr Murdoch took a slurp of tea and then looked her straight in the eye. "The wind farm is coming whether you, Pavel, or any bunch of deluded protestors like it or not. It's called progress."

Jenny couldn't swallow. Her throat had become dry.

"Without my dad," said Sandy, "none of you crofters would be able to stay here."

"Sandy," warned Mrs Murdoch once more.

The picture of her father lying on the beach, his face drained of colour and his eyes closed, flooded back into her mind. "I...

I wondered if I could call the hospital in Glasgow now. Just to see if my dad's all right."

Mr Murdoch eyed the cream-coloured phone that hung from the kitchen wall and sighed. "That's not going to be possible tonight, Jenny."

At first Jenny felt regret at speaking out so bluntly against the Murdochs. They were her hosts after all. But her regret soon changed into a tingle of fear that slithered round the back of her neck and down her spine. Mr Murdoch looked kind enough, but there was a darkness in his eyes that she couldn't fathom. "I thought you said it would be all right to phone, Mr Murdoch - back in the jeep." She wondered if the Murdochs were going to punish her now for saying too much, for simply saying what she believed.

Mr Murdoch hesitated. "Normally it would have been fine to use the phone, Jenny. No problem whatsoever but..."

Mrs Murdoch and Sandy both stared at Mr Murdoch, as if they, too, were interested to see how he would manage to palm her off.

"They took your father to the Vale of Leven Hospital at first, but he's been transferred to the Royal Alexandra in Paisley."

Mrs Murdoch screwed up her podgy face, mid-munch, and asked, "to the cardiology unit?"

"Yes, dear. I called them on the way here and it's best if we let them do their stuff just now."

"But he'll be worried about me and Lord," said Jenny. Her voice wavered. "He'll want to talk to me." Mr Murdoch avoided eye contact and resumed spooning extra gravy over his shepherd's pie.

"I told the staff nurse to let your father know, as soon as he wakes, that you're both safe and sound." Jenny could tell it was all a big lie.

Sandy Murdoch stifled a grin like someone in the know.

She would have to read the official-looking letter as soon as she could. She would go back home to her own house tonight.

"Not hungry any more?" asked Mrs Murdoch.

Jenny stared down at her half-eaten dinner. "No I'd..."

"I know," said Sandy, "you'd rather play us something on the piano."

"Your face is as white as a sheet," said Mrs Murdoch. "You've had a hard day."

"I'd like an early night, please. I feel a bit sick."

She waited for their response, for their permission.

"Off you go then," said Mr Murdoch.

"But dad," protested Sandy. "I wanted to hear her play Highland Cathedral."

"*Be quiet, Sandy.* Leave her alone," snapped Mrs Murdoch.

As Jenny climbed the stairs to the guest room, she could hear them talking about her in the kitchen. Sandy was moaning about missing her playing the piano. At the top of the landing she lingered a moment in front of the bedroom door, then pushed it open.

She froze on the spot.

Someone was sitting on her bed.

CHAPTER SEVEN
THE DECISION

The figure on the bed waved her into the room. "Come in and close the door, Jenny."

"Pavel?" gasped Jenny.

"Who did you think it was?" Pavel stood up and shut the door behind her.

"How did you get in here?" asked Jenny.

"They always leave the bedroom windows open. We live in Harris, Jenny, not London," Pavel reminded her. He had something in his hand. "I've read the letter."

Jenny flushed with anger. "You've no right to read my private things."

"Good job I did," said Pavel. He leaned across the bed and turned on the bedside light. "You've only two days left after tonight."

"Two days left for what?" said Jenny.

"How much money did you and your father need to stop the bank closing you down?"

Jenny was annoyed at the question. "It's none of your business."

"I'm on your side," said Pavel.

Jenny reached for the letter. "Give me it."

"How much did the bank ask you for?" he persisted, pulling the letter away from her. "How much to pay them off?"

"It was a huge amount. It was impossible..."

"Just tell me the number, Jenny."

Exasperated, Jenny glowered at the cheeky Polish boy sitting on her bed. Pavel was grinning but she did not feel like grinning back. "Twenty-two thousand pounds."

Pavel's cheeks dimpled as his smile stretched wider across his face. He opened the manila envelope and flicked the crease out of the white sheet of paper inside. He traced a line with his finger as he read to himself and then looked up at her. "Yep, I thought I'd read it right the first time. You'll get one hundred and eighty thousand pounds in change once you give the bank their money."

Jenny snatched the sheet of paper from Pavel's fingers and read it. She picked up the discarded manila envelope, peered inside and then held it upside down, shaking it vigorously. "There's no cheque in here." She re-read the letter. "Okay, so it says that they'll only issue the cheque when dad signs for it."

"Has the penny dropped yet, Jenny?" asked Pavel.

"What penny?"

"Why do you think Mr Murdoch has been keeping those letters from you? They were all from the same insurance company," said Pavel. "Two hundred and two thousand pounds. Whoah, you're rich."

Jenny was still staring at the letter. "It's mum's life insurance. She had cover after all. We never knew. If dad had known about this money he would have..."

"...told Mr Murdoch and the wind farm people to get lost?"

finished Pavel.

"Yes," said Jenny.

"And if Mr Murdoch keeps this information from your dad for another two days..." said Pavel.

"It will be too late," whispered Jenny. "The bank gave dad until noon on the thirtieth to clear his debts."

"It's the twenty-eighth," said Pavel.

"I have to phone the bank," said Jenny.

"And you think they'll believe a ten-year-old girl about a sudden windfall of two hundred and two thousand pounds?" said Pavel.

"I could confront the Murdochs, tell them that I found the letters. Just tell them to get me straight to Glasgow so that dad can sign for the money."

Pavel screwed up his face in disbelief. "You are kidding, right?" He took back the letter and carefully folded it into the manila envelope. "If you really want to save your farm without the need to have six massive turbines outside your back door, you must get your dad to sign this yourself. You need to get him to sign it and then you need to get it to the bank in Glasgow in the next two days."

Jenny plumped down on the bed beside Pavel. She clenched her fists and punched the pillow. "I hate the Murdochs. I bet every one of them is in on this."

"Perhaps... so what are you going to do?"

Jenny tried to calm down. She closed her eyes and began wrapping the tips of her long hair around her fingers. "So how would I get all the way to Glasgow?"

"Easy," said Pavel.

"But as soon as I disappear Mr Murdoch will call the police. He seems to know them all."

"He will, and he does," said Pavel. "That's why we have to go now."

"Both of us? Now?" Jenny was exhausted and had no idea how to get to Glasgow. She'd never been off the island in her whole life.

"You've got a hundred pounds in your purse," said Pavel.

"So Sandy was right," snapped Jenny, "you are a thief."

"Certainly not," protested Pavel, a hard-done-by expression forming on his face. "I didn't take your money. I just told you how much you have."

Jenny quickly checked her purse. Everything was in place. She stood up and walked over to the window. The moon had made a guest appearance between the rainclouds. "What's the plan, Pavel?"

"Well," mused Pavel, "if we leave right now and catch the six o'clock ferry from Tarbert we'll be in Uig by eight. Once we're on Skye, we'll-"

"We'll what?" asked Jenny.

"We'll take it from there," said Pavel, his cheeky smile returning. He placed his bony elbows on the windowsill beside Jenny's and looked out into the night. "The Murdochs don't get up until eight on a Saturday," he whispered.

"So there's a chance we'll get off the boat and on our way before they even realize we've gone," Jenny whispered back.

"What about you, Pavel? Will your father not miss you?"

"Nah," said Pavel. "Dad will be up doing all the things the Murdochs don't like doing on a Saturday morning. Besides," continued Pavel, "I've left a note to say that I've gone up to Stornoway to see my cousin, Willie Linky. I often go up there during the school holidays. That might just lead them North instead of South to Tarbert and the ferry."

Jenny tilted her head and checked the clock on the wall. It was after eleven. "How do we get to Tarbert from here? It must be…" she tried to calculate the distance in her head.

"Fifteen miles away," finished Pavel. "We can walk to the lambing shed. There's a quad bike parked up in the yard." He peered up at the sky. "The moon's bright enough. As long as the rain stays off a bit longer we should make it there with loads of time to spare."

"We'd better wait until the Murdochs go to sleep," said Jenny.

"No time like the present," said Pavel, another corny saying spilling from his lips.

"Are you sure?" said Jenny.

"Yep. Get your things." Pavel opened the window and the night air wafted into the bedroom. It ruffled the letter on the bed. "You'd better take the letter."

"You think?" said Jenny, sarcastically.

"I think," said Pavel. He grinned and shook his head. "This should be fun."

CHAPTER EIGHT
THE ESCAPE

Outside, Jenny slid down the slated incline until her shoes bumped onto the flat roof of the porch. Nervously, she glanced back up at the house.

Pavel placed his forefinger to his lips and then pointed to the top of a drainpipe a few feet ahead.

Jenny climbed over the rough felt until she gripped the top of the pipe. "Will it hold?" she whispered.

Pavel looked her up and down. "It held me, but I'm not too sure about you."

She gave him a swift punch to the arm.

"Hey," he moaned, rubbing his limb. "Come on." He helped Jenny over the edge of the roof and down the drainpipe.

A light flicked on above them. A shadow crossed over their faces.

"Sandy's room," said Pavel in a hushed voice. "Don't move. He's usually plugged into his X-box by this time."

There was a bark from Lord.

"Can we take Lord?" asked Jenny.

"No way," said Pavel. "It's going to be hard enough without having a dog in tow."

Jenny stared back up at Sandy's window. His outline wavered behind the glass for a few moments and then disappeared.

"Quickly," said Pavel, "before he comes back to the window." He snatched Jenny's hand and pulled her across the backyard. Their feet scrunched on the gravel and Lord yelped even louder. They had to duck behind an old ruined building at the edge of the Murdochs' garden. Jenny didn't like these old ruins. The remnants of the Harris whaling industry, they made her uneasy and sad at the same time. In the old days the whalers dragged the giant corpses up the beaches and then took the various parts of the poor beasts to these buildings for processing.

"This place gives me the creeps," said Jenny.

"Oil, soap and corsets," said Pavel, flippantly.

"Horrible," said Jenny.

Pavel stepped out of the ruin into the wet field beyond. "C'mon, the quad bike is just up that track."

As Jenny's eyes became more accustomed to the moonlight she began to slip and slide less frequently. A barn owl gave her the fright of her life as it glided across their path like a fleeting ghost. Her duffel bag was beginning to annoy her. It banged against her back as she struggled over a wooden spar fence.

"I can see the quad bike," said Pavel. "My dad always leaves the keys in the ignition."

As they moved through the lambing shed, Jenny could smell the ammonia from the sheep dip. She held her nose as she edged past the deep bath. "You still dip your sheep here?" she asked.

"It's cheaper," said Pavel. "We've got ticks all year round

now."

"It stinks," said Jenny.

"It doesn't even keep the ticks off for that long," said Pavel.

The lambing shed was deserted apart from a few rats that scuttled across the wisps of dirty straw at their feet.

Pavel whisked the tarpaulin off the quad bike.

"Jump aboard, me lady."

"You watch too much T.V.," said Jenny, stifling a smile. She looked down the hill at the Murdochs' house. Sandy's bedroom light was still on.

Like a dark monster, a dirty cloud edged across the sky. It blotted out the stars and then swallowed up the moon in one big gulp. The sea breeze strengthened as Jenny climbed onto the quad bike beside Pavel. "Won't they hear this thing starting up?" she asked.

"Nah," said Pavel. "We're well out of earshot and the wind is blowing up from the farm. It's okay." He turned the ignition key and pulled the gear out of neutral. The bike jerked forward and Jenny ducked as the barn owl returned to its roost. It was harder to see now that the moon had disappeared. She felt the unmistakable ping of a raindrop on her forehead.

"We're going to get wet," said Pavel.

Jenny could just make out a jumble of creepy stones ahead. They jutted out of the black earth beyond the faint outline of the railings. "Do we have to go past the graveyard?" she asked, her voice thin and listless.

"It's only the Murdochs," said Pavel. "Seven generations all stuffed into the one plot."

"Don't talk about it!" hissed Jenny. Her eyes were wide with fright.

"Jenny, do me a favour; jump off and open the gate. Just

watch out for the vampires and zombies behind that wall over there."

"Shut up!" she snapped. "You open the gate."

"Oh, for goodness sake," moaned Pavel. "I'm the driver, you're the gate-opener."

"No way," said Jenny.

Pavel stood up on the footrests and pointed at the eerie stones. "They're all dead. It won't take you more than a few seconds to..."

"No," snapped Jenny.

With a sigh of resignation, Pavel slipped down from the bike and walked up to the gate. He made a series of oohs and whooos, ghost-fashion, as he moved through the shadows. "Look out behind y... AH!"

Jenny screamed.

Raaar!

Something ran past Pavel's legs then jumped right up onto the seat beside her. "Get away!" She screamed again.

A long wet tongue covered her face in drool.

"LORD!" they both yelled.

CHAPTER NINE
TARBERT

Once they'd passed the small family graveyard, and a few more buildings left over from the days of the whaling station, it wasn't long before Jenny, Pavel and Lord reached the main road to Tarbert. Covered in new tarmac, and as smooth as glass, the road cut through an indiscernible carpet of thick heather and peaty lochans. As the moon reappeared, giant boulders and rocky outcrops cast long shadows across their path. The ghostly glow of the moon caught the surface of the road and allowed Pavel to turn off his giveaway lights. The quad bike purred along, sticking to the contours of the road for a further eight miles.

Jenny was pleased that Lord was with them. He seemed to be enjoying himself, nuzzling in between them on the double seat, his ears flattened, his tongue lolling beneath his silver-speckled jaw.

"There's Tarbert," said Pavel.

The yellow glow of the streetlights soon diluted the sharpness of the stars. The low angry clouds softened in the neon glare.

Jenny could see the ferry once they cleared the main

street. Its lights were on and it rose above the harbour like an oversized liquorice allsort, black and white with a red and yellow funnel. A few cars and lorries were lined up in the parking lanes.

"How are we going to do this?" asked Jenny.

"Do what?" said Pavel.

"Get the tickets and stuff."

Pavel drove the quad bike up the last incline in the road before the ferry car park and then killed the power.

Jenny gripped on a little tighter as the bike freewheeled into the shadows behind the public toilets.

"Right," said Pavel, stepping down from the quad bike, "we have two choices."

"Which are?" pressed Jenny.

"One: we buy the tickets ourselves when the ticket office opens at 5 a.m., or two: we sneak on board."

"How the heck can we sneak on board?" said Jenny. She watched Lord sniff around the base of a lamppost before lifting his leg.

Pavel scanned the car park. "Not much to hide in there. Let's just use your money and buy two tickets. It would be better if someone bought the tickets for us, though. We don't want to be remembered as 'that boy and girl with the dog, who came on by themselves'."

"Who's going to buy us a ticket?" asked Jenny. Pavel's attention seemed to be fixed on a silver BMW car. "That's got to be a rep's car," he murmured.

"What's a rep?" asked Jenny.

"A salesman, of course," said Pavel. "Why don't we ask him to get us the tickets? We'll just say that we're meeting our parents over on Skye. We'll just say that we're not sure how to buy tickets; you know, what to say and stuff."

Jenny called on Lord. "What about Lord?"

Pavel's shoulders dropped. "I suppose we'll have to take him with us. We can't exactly abandon him."

"No," said Jenny. "We can't." She cuddled into the old dog.

"The waiting room is open," said Pavel. "It's still empty and it will be warmer in there."

Jenny walked the short distance to the rickety old building and opened the door. It smelt of wet coats and pee. She plumped down onto a flaking maroon bench and watched Pavel as he stood on his tiptoes and switched on the heater. Her eyes were heavy and the single-element heater was soon enough to send her to sleep.

* * *

"Jenny?"

She woke with a gasp.

"The sales rep is coming towards the waiting room," said Pavel.

She yawned and rubbed her eyes. "What time is it?"

"Almost five," said Pavel.

The man walking towards them didn't look much older than them. It was beginning to get lighter and Jenny could see that he had neat brown hair and a wisp of a moustache. Seagulls scattered at his feet then took to the air in a blur of grey and white feathers. The remains of a fish supper lay strewn across his path. The man grimaced and sidestepped the mess.

Lord issued a low growl.

"He looks far too young to be a salesman," said Jenny, not

really sure what age you had to be to become a salesman in the first place. Her head was still muggy.

"Leave this to me," said Pavel.

Lord tugged on Pavel's belt, his makeshift lead. "Calm down, Lord," said Jenny.

Lord panted louder and then jerked forward. The lead slipped through Pavel's hand.

"Wait!" said Jenny.

Lord, however, was running full pelt at the young stranger.

Jenny watched the young man freeze and then brace.

Lord raced round the man's legs and made straight for the fish supper. Seagulls, already returning to their feast, squawked noisily as Lord snapped up at them. Soon, the old dog was munching down the greasy remnants of the takeaway.

The waiting room door swung inwards.

"Hi," said the man, in an upbeat voice. Chirpy, with kind eyes and very white teeth, he continued, "that's one hungry dog you've got there."

Jenny hesitated. "Yes..."

"He normally gets fed at the other side," said Pavel. "Our mum and dad are usually waiting with his stuff. This is Jean." He pointed to her.

Jean? thought Jenny. She supposed it was better not to use their real names. She nodded and then snuggled back into her coat, hoping Pavel would keep the rest of the conversation going.

"How did you get here so early?" said the man.

"We always get dropped off up there." Pavel pointed through the wall of the waiting room in the general direction of the main road.

"I thought this was the ticket office," said the man.

"Nah," Pavel stood up. "That's it across there." A light flickered on in the white portakabin as he said it.

Jenny noticed the light blue letters on the man's fleecy jacket: N.W.P.W.F.

"Jean's freezing and I'd better go and round up our mutt. I don't suppose I could ask you to get us a couple of tickets. Jean, give him the money."

Still not used to her new name, Jenny stared blankly for a moment before rummaging in her duffel bag.

"Don't your parents normally buy your tickets for you?" said the man.

"Normally," said Jenny, " but..."

"It's no problem," said the man. "I'll get you a couple of tickets."

Jenny was relieved. She'd had no idea how she was going to finish the sentence.

Pavel stepped outside, his belt-come-lead dangling from his hand. "Billy!" he yelled.

Billy, thought Jenny. *This is all getting very confusing.*

Lord, quite understandably, ignored Pavel and continued to scoff down the scattered chips.

As the man turned to leave, Jenny asked, "what do the letters on your jacket stand for?"

The young man hovered in the doorway.

"These?" he pointed to the light blue embroidered letters. "They stand for: North West Power Wind Farms."

"Oh," squeaked Jenny, suddenly wishing she'd never asked.

CHAPTER TEN
BOATS AND BIRDS

After negotiating the gangplank, or whatever it was called, Jenny moved, as she'd been instructed, in beside an elderly couple. Pavel and Lord followed suit.

Pavel had suggested that they try to blend in with the other passengers as much as possible.

Because they had Lord with them, however, they ended up being restricted to the main area beside the purser's office.

"Dogs aren't allowed anywhere else inside the ship," explained Pavel.

"Well, let's go outside then," said Jenny. "I've never been on a boat before."

Pavel slumped. "But it's freezing and..."

Jenny put on her best 'I'm just about to cry' face.

"Fine," moaned Pavel, scanning the other passengers. "Don't put on that face, Jenny. They'll think I'm being mean to you."

"You are," said Jenny.

Pavel sighed and pushed open the heavy door that led out to the deck.

It was already light, and Jenny rested her elbows and chin

on the wooden railing as they edged out of the inlet. She felt the vibration of the boat run through her. Gulls and seals sat motionless on slate-grey rocks that dripped with seaweed. Pavel pointed out a giant skua.

To Jenny, it looked like a massive brown seagull, but Pavel explained that it was a close relation of the albatross and that it ate other birds' chicks.

"That's horrible," said Jenny.

"That's the circle of life," replied Pavel.

"Just how many of those stupid sayings and phrases do you know?" said Jenny.

Pavel laughed, his freckles wrinkling together. "Thousands. This is the way that I learned your language."

"Gaelic is my language," reminded Jenny.

"You know what I mean," said Pavel. "When we first came here from Poland, we lived near Glasgow. It was pretty tough."

"What do you mean by 'tough'?" asked Jenny, her eyes still fixed on the flurry of foam that formed lace-like patterns around the hull of the ferry.

Pavel took a deep breath. "I didn't speak a word of English, and they just put me into school."

"So what did you do?" asked Jenny.

"I learned to survive. I learned to read people's faces, some basic words and stuff and then I found a book of sayings. The other kids laughed when I tried to say them in my accent, but that was better than being bullied."

"They hurt you?"

"Sometimes," said Pavel.

"Were they worse than Sandy Murdoch?"

"Much worse." Pavel rolled up his sleeve and showed Jenny a scar on his arm.

"You're kidding," she gasped.

"No," said Pavel.

"There was a boy called Flynn, who was just plain evil." Pavel shrugged. "Still – all's fair in love and war."

"That wasn't fair at all," said Jenny.

"I suppose not. Anyway, after that," Pavel rolled his sleeve back down, "we moved here."

"So are all the Glasgow kids like that? I mean nasty and stuff," asked Jenny.

Pavel laughed. "No, don't tar them all with the same brush."

Jenny screwed up her face and then said, "That's another stupid saying, isn't it?"

"Not so stupid," said Pavel. "Mostly, Glasgow is a great place. Flynn was just a bad egg."

"He sounds horrible," said Jenny.

As the ferry moved along the inlet and out into the Minch, Jenny craned up at the red and yellow funnel. "How does something this big and heavy even float?"

Pavel laughed again. "I don't know, but I'm glad it does."

"Are you two not cold out here?" said a familiar voice.

The young man who'd bought their tickets was walking along the green-painted deck towards them.

"Not really," said Pavel. "What about you, just getting a breath of fresh air?"

"Something like that." The young man smiled and offered his hand. "My name's Brad, Brad Miller, but everyone just calls me Windy."

Jenny smiled and shook his hand. Pavel was smirking. "Windy?"

"Do you fancy some breakfast?" asked Windy.

"But what about Lord?" blurted Jenny.

Pavel frowned at her.

"Lord?" said Windy.

"She means Billy," said Pavel. "Very religious, our *Jean*. Always saying little prayers in her head."

"Oh, yes, very religious," stuttered Jenny, knowing fine well that she'd never been to church since her mother passed away.

"Tell you what," said Windy. "We all know that Billy has had his breakfast, so how about I bring you a couple of bacon rolls. That way you don't have to leave the doggy zone. What do you say?"

"Fine," said Pavel.

Jenny wasn't sure that she could keep up the lies all through a breakfast with Windy.

Windy gave them the thumbs up and disappeared back into the boat.

"How weird is that," said Pavel, "him being called Windy?"

"He works for the wind farm people," explained Jenny. "The letters on his jacket..."

"Brilliant," said Pavel, a serious look forming on his face. "You're joking?"

It was much warmer inside the boat. Lord, or Billy, as they now had to call him, soon fell asleep at their feet and their bacon rolls arrived on a plastic tray.

"There you go," said Windy.

Jenny wondered what age he was. His legs were pretty gangly and he had a clumsy way about him. He spilled half of his tea over his lap and burst a biro pen, all in about ten seconds.

"There," he said, finally. "This bacon roll is just the job." He took a bite and ended up with three inches of bacon rind and a dollop of tomato sauce on his black trousers.

Jenny giggled.

"So you build wind turbines," said Pavel.

"Mmm..." said Windy, his mouth still full.

"They gave...me...my...first...job..." He finally swallowed and sighed.

"So, you're not worried about the effect the windmills have on the bird life?" asked Pavel.

Jenny's smile faded. She thought that this kind of question was very rude of Pavel, especially since Windy had just bought them breakfast. "I'm sorry," she said, grimacing at Pavel.

"No...no, it's a fair question," said Windy, his face becoming more serious, too. "You're worried about...?"

"Two things, really," said Pavel. "Firstly, the scarecrow effect and secondly, the arms actually hitting birds."

Windy looked quite taken aback. "Yes, well, you've done your homework," said Windy. "Sorry, what was your name again?"

"Tom," said Pavel, quite unconvincingly.

"Well, Tom, it's a bit of a balancing act, isn't it?"

"Is it?" answered Pavel.

"Well, yes," said Windy.

Pavel took a slurp of tea before saying, "This scarecrow effect: they reckon that windmills scare off birds for miles around, stop them nesting."

Windy considered this for a few moments and then said, "The turbines, or windmills, as you put it, seem to have an effect on some species, but not all. And they would only have an effect on nesting for, say, half a mile, and..."

"And that's all right then, is it?" snapped Pavel.

Jenny cringed.

"You have to be careful where you site them," explained Windy.

Pavel straightened in his seat. "What about that windmill in America? I read about it on the Internet. It kills more than thirteen hundred birds of prey every year."

"Again," stressed Windy, "that's down to where you put them."

"You can see why people are worried on our island," said Jenny, in a conciliatory tone.

"Of course you can," said Windy. "But tell me this: how much more damage to those birds and us might there be if we continue to ignore global warming? Have you any idea how much the sea level is due to rise?"

"I suppose there is that," mused Jenny.

"We don't even know if that's what's really going to happen, do we?" said Pavel. He gave Jenny a stern look.

"Such big questions," said Windy. "All I know is that I joined this wind farm company to help the planet, not to do more damage."

"What do you do, exactly?" asked Jenny, maintaining her more friendly tone.

"It's my job to find the best sites," said Windy. Somewhere you can reach the 'Betz Limit'."

"The what?" asked Pavel.

"The 'Betz Limit' is the exact place where the maximum energy can be extracted from the turbine. A few yards either way can make a massive difference. But..." Windy slipped a copy of 'The Pocket Guide to British Birds' from his jacket pocket. "It has to be somewhere with the least environmental impact." He waved the book and smiled.

Just then, a tannoy announcement echoed across the boat: "We regret that due to an unforeseen technical problem, we will be diverting to Lochmaddy, on the Isle of Uist. Estimated time of arrival in Uig is now, 11 a.m."

As Windy flicked through the pages of his bird book, Pavel caught Jenny's eye. She could tell they were in big trouble.

CHAPTER ELEVEN
LOCHMADDY

With Windy busy on his mobile, Pavel and Jenny got a chance to talk.

"The Murdochs will find out I've run off and then they'll phone the police," said Jenny.

"Who, in turn, will phone the captain of this ferry," said Pavel.

Jenny felt the tears welling up inside her.

"Try to keep calm, Jenny," said Pavel, eyeing his fellow passengers.

"I can't keep calm, so don't ask me to," snapped Jenny.

Pavel backed off and tried to shush Lord, who had begun a low rumbling growl.

"I need to speak to my dad, Pavel. I need to know that he's all right."

Pavel looked agitated. "What hospital did the Murdochs say he was in?"

Jenny tried her best to remember, but she couldn't. "I can't remember."

"Yes you can. Think," said Pavel.

Jenny began to cry. "It sounded like..."

"Like what?" pressed Pavel.

"It sounded like a girl's name!" Jenny sniffed.

"The hospital sounds like a girl's name?" Pavel closed his eyes and scratched his head. "Right, here's what we can do."

Jenny dried her eyes with the hem of her coat.

Nearly everyone on the ferry was trying to get a signal on their mobile to make new arrangements.

"What's your plan, Pavel?" said Jenny.

"A bird in the hand is worth two in the bush," said Pavel.

"Which means?" sniffed Jenny.

"Lochmaddy is our 'bird in the hand'," said Pavel.

"Eh?" Jenny was none-the-wiser.

"If we get off the ferry at Lochmaddy, we know we'll be off the radar. The Murdochs' radar, that is. We'll be on dry land by eight, which means that it will be too late for the Murdochs to sound the alarm."

"Then what?" asked Jenny.

"Simple. We get down the chain of islands. Lochmaddy is on North Uist. After that, we travel down to Benbecula and then it's on to South Uist and the next ferry we need to catch at Lochboisdale."

"And where does that one go?" asked Jenny.

"It depends. It might be Barra, and then on to Oban," said Pavel.

"Tom!" It was Windy, and Pavel was ignoring him again.

Jenny caught him by the sleeve. "I wish you hadn't changed all our names, it really makes life a lot..."

"You two okay?" interrupted Windy.

"Oh, ah, yes," said Pavel.

Windy sat down and patted Lord. "This totally ruins my connections to Oban."

"Same here," said Pavel.

"Won't your mother and father wait a couple of extra hours for you?"

"Normally they would have," explained Pavel. "But our dad's got an interview in Oban today."

Jenny was amazed at Pavel's ability to lie so effortlessly.

"Don't suppose we could borrow your phone?" continued Pavel.

Windy beamed. "You can try it. So you need to be in Oban too?"

"That's where we were going anyway," said Pavel.

He took the phone. "Give us a minute, Windy. There might be a solution for us all."

"There might?" said Windy.

Pavel placed the end of Lord's lead in Windy's hand and led Jenny into the cafeteria.

"Now what?" whispered Jenny.

"I dial directory inquiries," said Pavel, "and ask for all the hospitals that begin with a girl's name in Glasgow. I say them out loud and you nod when you hear the one that your dad's in."

Jenny's heart raced. "Okay." She watched Pavel dial and then turn the corner. By the time she caught him up he was already speaking to someone. He shook his head and pressed the phone off.

"What's going on," asked Jenny.

Pavel was punching in more numbers. She heard him ask for the operator. She made to speak but he waved his hand for her to be quiet.

"Not another one. What do you mean you can only give me two numbers? Yes... well, can you text me a list...? Hello? Can you hear me?" He shook the mobile and placed it back to his ear. He sighed and handed the phone to Jenny. "Two useless operators and now the reception's gone again."

Jenny felt her stomach flutter. "Everything is against us."

"No it isn't," said Pavel. He marched off in the direction of the purser's office and began studying the list of ferry timetables. His finger trailed down the column of numbers until it wavered over one line. "Here it is," he said. "If we get off at Lochmaddy, there's a connecting bus to Lochboisdale. Then, all we have to do is catch the ferry from there to Oban. It's a straight run. We'll actually be ahead of schedule and still under the Murdoch radar."

"Fine," sniffed Jenny.

Windy was walking towards them.

Pavel shook his head mournfully and handed back the mobile. "Got cut off again."

Windy examined his phone. "And now it's out of power. Guess what?" he continued, "I've checked with the crew, and I can take my car off at Lochmaddy."

"So you can catch the ferry from Lochboisdale to Oban," added Pavel.

Windy beamed. "Exactly."

"Can we come with you?" said Jenny. She knew it was a silly question the instant it left her lips.

"Well..." Windy hesitated, "you don't even know me and... Jean, what would your parents think of you jumping into a stranger's car?"

"Look," said Pavel, "before the phone went dead, dad told us to get on the ferry to Oban. We'll be going the same way anyway."

Windy's expression hardened. "I'm not comfortable with

the idea of giving you a lift. If I could have spoken to your father first, explained things a bit more..."

"We can get the bus," said Jenny.

"Yeah, we can get the connecting bus," confirmed Pavel.

Jenny looked at Windy's tight-lipped expression and wished again that she'd never opened her mouth. She could smell a mixture of diesel and breakfast. There was something strangely warm and nice about it and it took her mind off Pavel's risky lies.

The ferry made a funny noise. Jenny could see houses and a hotel through the porthole in the door.

As they pulled alongside the harbour, Pavel pointed out the bus stop.

"Let's meet up on the Oban ferry, have some lunch," said Windy.

"Well, as long as you're sure you won't get arrested," said Pavel, a cheeky grin on his freckled face.

Jenny punched Pavel on the arm. "Ouch!"

"He can be annoying sometimes," she explained to Windy.

Windy just shook his head and opened the door that led down to the car deck. "I'd better get going."

Once Windy had gone, Pavel turned to Jenny and sighed. "You can't get blood from a stone."

"What?" said Jenny, the breeze ruffling her hair. "You mean Windy wouldn't have taken us no matter what lies you told him?"

"Something like that," said Pavel.

They shuffled down the gangway and onto the harbour side before Jenny spotted a red and white bus with an array of glowing yellow dots that formed the word, 'Lochboisdale'. She nudged Pavel. A few extra dots were peppered round the first

'L'. "Look's like we're going to 'Oochboisdale'.

Pavel smiled.

With a blast from the funnel, the black and white ferry raised its green ramp and edged away from the pier in a gurgle of bubbles.

Jenny cuddled into Lord. She was pleased the old dog had come. She swung her duffel bag over her shoulder.

"He's a nice bloke, that Windy, despite working for the enemy," said Pavel.

Jenny thought this was a strange thing for Pavel to say. "He's not the enemy," she said. "He's just doing his job. In his mind, he's doing good."

"In his mind," muttered Pavel.

"It's mean to call him 'the enemy'. He bought us breakfast and gave us a loan of his phone. He was a nice man."

As they waited to board the bus, a police car edged round the bend onto the road ahead.

"Quick," said Pavel. "Get behind the bus shelter."

Jenny pulled Lord round into the mud and reeds.

The Police car slowed and then pulled up next to the harbour, opposite the hotel.

"What time is it?" asked Jenny.

Pavel looked down at his watch. "Almost 8.30. We need to assume the Murdochs know you've gone."

They watched two policemen talking to a few of the men who worked for the ferry company.

The bus revved.

"We'd better get on," said Pavel. "We'll have to risk it."

"We can't," said Jenny, in a small voice.

"Why not? We need to get on now," urged Pavel.

"I... I left..."

"What is it, Jenny?"
"I left my purse on the ferry," she whimpered.

CHAPTER TWELVE
PANIC AT HILLTOP

As the police car moved towards them, Jenny and Pavel had to sneak back round the side of the bus shelter again to keep out of view.

"Are you quite finished?"

Jenny and Pavel peered round the side of the shelter.

The bus driver was staring down at them. "You know, there are public toilets at the ticket office." He pointed back at the ferry terminal.

"No," bleated Jenny. "We weren't... It was the dog."

"Well I hope you cleaned it up. Just because this is an island in the middle of nowhere doesn't mean we don't tidy up that kind of thing."

Jenny stared up at him blankly.

"Well, are you getting on the bus or not?" pressed the driver. He had a chubby, weather-beaten face and wore a black-rimmed hat that was far too small for him. His pig-like eyes blinked as he waited for an answer.

"We want to get on," began Pavel.

"But I've left my purse on the boat," finished Jenny.

"Sure you have," said the driver. "A couple of chancers,

eh?"

"No, it's the truth," said Jenny, in the most pathetic 'little-girl-lost' voice she could muster.

"And you've got a mutt with you," said the driver. He pushed the rim of his hat further up his forehead and shook his head.

"His name is Lord," said Jenny.

Pavel poked her in the ribs but it was too late. She'd just blurted out Lord's name and that was that.

The driver tilted his head and looked hard at Lord. "Very high and mighty, I'm sure. And you say you've no money whatsoever."

With a reluctant sigh, Pavel dug into his trouser pocket and produced a wrinkled five-pound note. "I only have this." He offered it to the driver, who unravelled it with a look of disgust on his face.

"Well, I can't exactly refuse to give you a lift with a dog named Lord now, can I? It wouldn't be right. Besides, a child's fare is only one pound twenty. You'll have enough change for a packet of crisps on the ferry at the other end. I take it you want to catch the ferry to Oban?"

Jenny nodded.

The driver punched a few numbers into his machine and two pink tickets emerged from a small hole. "The dog's free of charge," he added.

"Thanks," said Jenny.

"My pleasure, mademoiselle," he replied.

They shuffled up to the back of the bus and sat down.

Although Jenny was tired, hungry and worried about her father, she still felt a tingle of excitement. She'd never been on such a journey before, never been so far from home and there was something else... *Was it danger?* she wondered. *Was she beginning to enjoy the risks and the lies?* A feeling of dread spun round in her stomach like a big heavy coat in a washing machine. It put her off kilter, made her heart race. As the bus jolted forward, however, she thought about her father lying in some unknown bed in some unknown hospital, alone.

She slumped back into her seat and dropped her duffel bag on the floor.

"Let me check your bag again," said Pavel.

As Jenny listened to Pavel pulling and hauling at her bag, her eyes drifted over the other passengers. There were two old ladies with matching bobbled hats that looked like tea cosies; a middle-aged man in a boiler suit; and a very neat-looking gent with a shiny briefcase and a natty tie. Jenny had noticed the tie as she'd passed, gold with lots of animals on it.

Another dig in the ribs from Pavel snapped her out of her thoughts.

"The police car's coming towards us," he said, in an urgent whisper.

Jenny watched the car roll past the bus and then pull off the road onto a raised piece of ground ahead.

Pavel pulled her down in her seat as the bus moved closer.

Jenny could see that the driver was watching them in the rear view mirror.

Once they were a good fifty yards away from the police car, they turned and knelt up on the back seats, squinting through the head rests for any sign of a flashing blue light. Lord followed suit, barking at the police car as it faded into the distance.

Pavel began stuffing Jenny's things back into the duffel bag, but Jenny caught his hand. "I'll do it," she said, glowering at her tall companion. He was an accomplished liar, cheeky and impulsive, but she liked him. She felt safe with him. He would get her to her father. She just knew it.

* * *

At Hilltop Farm, Mr Murdoch's black jeep skidded to a halt on the gravel outside. He leapt out and pushed open the front door.

"Any sign of her?" he asked.

"Not a jot," said Mrs Murdoch. "I knocked her door to see if she wanted any breakfast, and when there was no answer I took a look inside the bedroom, but..."

"I know," said Mr Murdoch, briskly, "you told me. Gone, along with her bag and her stupid dog."

"Are you going to check Hushwish?" asked Mrs Murdoch.

"Yes, yes," he hissed.

"Well, you don't have to snap my head off," she complained.

Distractedly, Mr Murdoch moved into the living room.

Mrs Murdoch followed. "What are you doing now?"

"I need to check on something." He began pulling sheets of music from the piano stool. "SANDY!" he roared.

Mrs Murdoch felt her mouth become dry. "What is it, Angus? She's probably just run back to her own farm. Jenny's headstrong like her father. Why are you rummaging about in there?"

"SANDY!" Mr Murdoch roared again, ignoring her.

She watched him slam the lid of the piano stool shut and then march back into the hall. She caught his arm. "Angus?"

"I can't explain just now," he snapped.

Sandy appeared, bleary-eyed, at the top of the stairs.

"I thought I told you to keep an eye on her, boy."

"Keep an eye on who?" Sandy pulled a black t-shirt over his head. He wriggled his arms into the sleeves as he stumbled down the steps.

Angus Murdoch shook his head mournfully and sighed. "See. This is what I have to put up with."

"Don't be so hard on him, Angus," said Mrs Murdoch.

"Hard on him?" He pulled her into the kitchen and sat her down.

Shaken, Mrs Murdoch tried to read his face.

"Look, Ellen, we could lose our farm, everything, if we don't find Jenny quickly."

"I don't see how," she said.

"It's complicated," said Angus. "Sandy and I will keep looking on the island for a while. You wait here in case she turns up."

"But Angus, I don't see how that wee girl could lose us everything. You're over-reacting."

Angus pushed his face closer to hers. "I can assure you, I'm not."

Ellen's hands slid off the edge of the kitchen table. Her brow was moist. "What have you done, Angus?"

Sandy Murdoch burst into the kitchen, a toothbrush jutting from his mouth. He tried to speak, "She's... gone, dwad." A lump of toothpaste plopped onto his shirt.

Angus shook his head. "Nice one, Sherlock. Now get a bag packed and get moving. We might be going to Glasgow."

"Glasgow?" said Sandy.

"Why do you repeat everything I say, like an imbecile?"

"An imbecile?" Sandy yawned.

Angus Murdoch shook his head again and pulled a holdall from the kitchen cupboard.

"Just do as your father says," said Mrs Murdoch. She'd never seen Angus this uptight before. Her mind was racing with all sorts of horrible scenarios.

"Where's Pavel?" said Sandy.

"Where, indeed," said his dad. "There's no sign of him either."

In minutes, Angus and Sandy were in the jeep and skidding out of the driveway.

Ellen slumped down into a kitchen chair and stared, shell-shocked, at the family picture on the fridge door. It showed the three of them, tanned and happy, standing on the beach in Javea. *Would their Spanish villa be under threat too?*

There was a knock at the front door.

She sniffed and steadied herself on the kitchen table for a moment before getting up. She pulled the door open.

"Mrs Murdoch?"

The postman stood on her step, a big parcel in his hands.

"Morning, Charlie," she sighed. It was rare for Charlie to turn up on the step. Angus usually caught him first.

"Everything all right, Mrs Murdoch?"

"Oh, yes," she lied.

"I nearly forgot," said Charlie, "there's another letter for the MacLeods."

Ellen Murdoch wrinkled her brow and studied the manila-coloured envelope.

"I usually see Mr Murdoch at the cattle shed, but he wasn't there this morning. Sorry to disturb you."

"That's all right," she said, in a small voice. She waved goodbye to Charlie, without once taking her eyes off of the letter.

CHAPTER THIRTEEN
SOUTH UIST

The bus bumped and jiggled along the single-track road that stretched south. Past brackish lochans and sweeping white beaches, across man-made causeways and in and out of passing places, they continued down the backbone of North Uist until they reached the middle island of the Southern Hebrides – Benbecula. Here, the bus picked up a group of school children and someone who, Jenny presumed, was their teacher.

After this brief stop the bus purred onwards once again, skirting ruined castles and green meadows full of flowers. The sea would disappear for a while and then reappear, as blue as it was back in Hushwish Bay, teeming with birds and laced with foaming waves.

The sky was clear now and as deep a blue as Jenny had ever seen. She imagined it went on forever, out into space and beyond the stars. She closed her eyes and tried to picture her father. She imagined him looking out of some hospital window at the same magical sky, thinking of Lord and her. *We're coming, Dad, we're coming, she thought. And we'll keep our beautiful bay the way it has always been.*

"Jenny MacLeod," said a woman's voice.

Pavel, who'd dosed off, woke up with a start.

Jenny screwed up her eyes and stared down the bus. It was the teacher who'd just boarded with the school children. She was fair-skinned with caramel-coloured hair and a lean frame. Her cheekbones were very pronounced, striking, and eyes were almost as blue as the sea. She had a kind smile.

"Yes," answered Jenny.

Pavel issued a sigh of exasperation and slumped back into his seat. "Brilliant."

"It's been three years but I was sure it was you," said the woman.

Jenny forced a smile and racked her brains. *Who is this woman?*

"I knew your mother, Catherine. I was very sad to hear that she'd... well, I was very sad," said the woman, a flush of pink finding her cheeks.

She nodded at Pavel and then sat down on a seat one row from the back.

Lord wagged his tail and Jenny peered at the school children. They were a bit younger than her, perhaps eight or nine.

The woman followed Jenny's gaze. "Oh, they'll behave themselves for a moment."

"I don't remember," began Jenny.

"Don't remember me? No, maybe not." She gave Jenny a sympathetic smile. "Before I became a teacher, I worked in the doctor's surgery in Stornoway."

Jenny didn't ask which one. Her mother had visited quite a few before she eventually believed what they all told her.

"Where are you off to?" asked the woman.

Pavel patted Jenny on the arm, as if to say – be quiet now, I'll take over from here… but Jenny thought that the woman had kind eyes and blurted out, "Glasgow."

Pavel cleared his throat and added, "To Oban first, though."

Jenny didn't think this was any better than what she'd said.

"And you?" She stared over the lady's shoulder at the children further down the bus.

"Oh, we're off at the next stop. It's the Saturday Club. We're going to visit a stone circle. It's been nice to see you, Jenny. Tell your father I was asking for him." The woman edged off her seat and patted Lord on the head before returning to her group of kids.

The bus slowed.

The woman with the caramel-coloured hair ushered the children off the bus and whispered something to the driver, before turning to wave up at them one last time.

"She's told him it's us," hissed Pavel. "Caught, like rats in a trap. Nice one, Jenny."

"Don't be a numpty. She knew me," said Jenny, "and she knew my Mum."

"She only thought she knew you. She wasn't sure," said Pavel. He strained to see what the bus driver was doing.

Jenny felt the anger inside her build. "If you stick your neck out like a giraffe, he's bound to get suspicious."

"I just want to see if he's got a mobile."

"If we're caught, we're caught," snapped Jenny. "I'm getting tired of lying and…"

Pavel found her hand and looked into her eyes. "I thought you wanted to find your father? I thought that you wanted to save your farm, your beautiful bay?"

"I do," said Jenny, in an urgent whisper, "but I don't know

if I can keep running and hiding and..."

"You're doing fine," relented Pavel. "I'm sorry."

The bus slowed once more as they passed a sign that said 'Lochboisdale'.

Pavel found the end of Lord's lead. "The ferry's in the harbour, look."

Jenny picked up her green duffel bag.

"I'll take the bag," said Pavel. "You take Lord."

"But how are we going to get on board. We've no money," said Jenny.

They shuffled down between the seats until they reached the bus driver.

"Good luck," he said.

Jenny smiled and said goodbye. The driver seemed different now, more sympathetic and less cheeky.

Pavel stepped off the bus and walked towards a row of houses.

Jenny waited until Lord skidded off the bus and followed. "Where are you going, Pavel?" The ferry was in the opposite direction.

Pavel ducked up a dark close next to a row of black plastic trolley-bins.

She followed.

"We can see the ferry traffic from here," he said, "and I think we have three options."

"Which are?" pressed Jenny, feeling hungry and fed up again.

In a calm voice, Pavel began, "There's a pickup with a horse box, a lorry load of sheep and Windy's BMW."

"I say we go straight to Windy and tell him I've lost my purse."

"I say we don't," said Pavel, not once taking his eyes off the row of traffic. "That would just make him suspicious."

"He's not the enemy, Pavel," said Jenny.

"Mmm..." Pavel mused, "I say we sneak onto the lorry with the sheep."

"Now that's just stupid. Lord would drive them crazy and we'd get covered in..."

"Well," interrupted Pavel. "There is always option number four."

"Which is?" sighed Jenny.

"That lorry right there."

Jenny saw a big lorry with a green canvas cover. She could see that the cover was loose at one corner. The car directly behind it was empty and the driver of the lorry was busy tapping his steering wheel to some unknown beat.

"C'mon, then," said Pavel. He grabbed her arm and hauled her towards the lorry. Before Jenny could get angry with him, Pavel had reached the green cover and flicked it open. He leapt up onto the lorry and then reached round to grab hold of Jenny's hand.

Lord bounded up beside Pavel as Jenny scrambled onto the trailer.

Pavel flicked the cover back down and everything went dark.

As Jenny's eyes became accustomed to the dim green light she soon saw that they were standing at the edge of a tangle of wooden trusses and frames.

"I reckon it's a kit house," said Pavel.

"Like the Murdochs'?" said Jenny.

"Yeah," said Pavel. "Let's move into the middle, in case anyone checks in here."

Jenny heard the lorry's engine roar as it moved forward. She gripped onto a spar of wood and pulled herself along until she reached Pavel. She braced as the lorry pitched forward and then began to climb. "We must be going inside the ferry," she whispered.

"And for free," said Pavel. "Let's wait another ten minutes and then we'll slip out of here and up onto the deck. We don't want to be stuck in here the whole trip. It's more than five hours long according to the timetable on the last ferry."

Jenny closed her eyes and patted Lord. "I don't know if it's because I can't see anything, but I'm beginning to feel sick."

"Brilliant," said Pavel.

"I don't like confined spaces," said Jenny.

Pavel looked at his watch. "Let's go now then."

They made their way back through the wooden spars until they reached the point where they'd entered the wagon. Jenny tugged at the canvas cover. "It's stuck."

"Let me try," said Pavel. He pulled and heaved for a few seconds but it still didn't budge. "Great, the driver's probably secured it."

"I don't feel good, Pavel," whimpered Jenny.

"Keep calm. Patience is a virtue."

"Don't even start with those stupid sayings or I'll kick you."

Pavel slipped his hand into his jacket.

"What's that?" asked Jenny, but she could see it was a knife.

"It's a lamb's-foot knife. Razor sharp." Pavel pierced the canvas and cut a diagonal slice in the fabric. He cut another slash to form a cross and then pushed the material outward. A triangular hole appeared.

Jenny could see the side of a shiny blue Land Rover. She

peeked out. "There's nobody about."

"Jump down now," urged Pavel.

There was a deep blast of a foghorn.

Jenny edged down onto the metal deck and began wandering through the parked cars. She looked back for Pavel and saw him pulling a lace from his shoe. He pierced two neat holes in the canvas and stitched the lace through, pulling it tight until the gap in the material disappeared.

"There," he said, triumphantly.

Jenny shook her head. "You've done that before, haven't you?"

Pavel gave her a knowing smile.

Jenny saw a metal door swing shut a few yards ahead of them.

"We're too late," said Pavel.

"Well, if you hadn't been busy knitting we could have made it."

"It's always good to cover your tracks. We might have to go off the ferry the same way we came on.

"You there!"

Jenny turned.

A tall man was walking towards them.

CHAPTER FOURTEEN
MCGOVERN

The man, who wore a pair of white overalls and carried a can of white paint, looked surprised to see them. "Where's your car?"

Jenny jerked her thumb backwards at the side of her right ear.

"We were sent down for the dog," said Pavel. The man stared down at Lord. "Well, whoever sent you almost got you locked in the car deck for five hours." The man shook his head mournfully. "Parents these days." He tilted his head and half closed his eyes. Staring at Pavel, he asked, "So, where are you from, originally, boy?"

Jenny thought this was a rude question.

Pavel, however, just smiled. "I'm from Poland."

"He's my best friend," added Jenny.

"Half the staff on this ruddy ferry are from somewhere like that," said the man. He muttered something about wages and foreigners, but Jenny couldn't hear him properly.

"We've never been on a ferry before," she lied.

She didn't like this man's attitude and she thought changing the subject might stop him from looking at Pavel so strangely.

The man sighed and placed his paint pot on a metal spar. He stabbed his long thin brush into the paint and began checking his pockets. He produced a bunch of keys and led them to the heavy metal door. "I've a good mind to come up there and have a word with your father."

"Oh, don't worry," said Pavel, "Jean here's got a temper on her. She'll give him what for."

"I wasn't talking to you, son," said the man in a sinister tone.

Pavel shrugged and pulled Lord into his leg.

Jenny wanted away from this man as quickly as possible. He was turning out to be a nasty piece of work.

As soon as the door opened wide enough, they raced past him and up the stairs. Lord skidded on the smooth steps, panting as he pulled Pavel further ahead of her.

At the top of the stairs, Jenny and Pavel slumped onto one of the big leatherette seats.

"He was horrid to you," said Jenny.

"He had a chip on his shoulder," said Pavel.

"Sometimes people are like that."

"I've never seen anyone act like that before."

Tight-lipped, Pavel shrugged his shoulders again.

"He was racist," said Jenny.

"Who was racist?" said a familiar voice.

"Windy!" cried Jenny, pleased to see their lanky friend.

"Oh, it was nothing," said Pavel.

"Racism isn't 'nothing'." He eyed Pavel. "Was someone bothering you, Tom?"

"No," said Pavel. "We just overheard some people on the bus."

Jenny could tell that Pavel didn't want to talk about it.

Windy's face lightened a little. "Well, just as long as..."

"What's the forecast, Windy?" interrupted Jenny.

Windy sat down beside them and opened an Ordinance Survey map. "It's supposed to get rough down at Tiree," he said. He stabbed his finger into the chart. "Right there."

Jenny squinted to see where he was pointing. She knew Tiree was an island to the south of Barra. She'd had to endure Sandy Murdoch's boasts about surfing off its beaches. His dad paid for special lessons.

"When I couldn't find you on the deck earlier, I thought you might have skipped the ferry," said Windy. "I wasn't sure you'd have the money to get on."

Jenny saw him reach into the pocket of his fleece. "Found this on the floor of the last ferry. Right where your duffel bag had been." He held up her purse.

"Oh, thank goodness," gasped Jenny. She gave Pavel a withering look.

"What?" said Pavel.

Windy got up and walked over to the shop. As soon as he was out of sight Jenny whacked Pavel on the arm.

"Ouch! What is it with you?" Pavel rubbed the top of his arm. "You've given me a dead arm."

"Good," said Jenny. "I told you we should have walked straight up to Windy's car."

"Hindsight is a wonderful thing," said Pavel,

She punched him in the arm again. "And that's for spouting out another stupid saying."

Pavel stood up, open-mouthed. "You really need an anger-management class."

Jenny bristled. "And you need to listen to me sometimes."

"Okay, keep your hair on," whined Pavel. "Behave, here

comes Windy again."

Windy handed them both an ice cream.

Jenny's stomach tingled in anticipation. "Thanks, Windy." She nudged Pavel.

"Yeah, thanks," he added.

Jenny wondered if Pavel still considered Windy 'the enemy'. He was just as narrow-minded as the stupid man down on the car deck, she decided. In fact, the way she felt about Pavel right at that moment made her wonder about telling Windy everything: her father's collapse; the protestors; the Murdochs; the letter; the whole lot.

"So how did you pay for your tickets," asked Windy.

Jenny took a large bite of her ice cream and stared hard at Pavel.

"I just had enough...to...cover it," said Pavel, in between licks.

"Yes, Pavel had..." Jenny stopped mid sentence, but it was too late.

"Pavel?" asked Windy.

Pavel's face was a picture. Ice cream dripped from his chin onto the red carpet that covered the deck.

"Are you okay, Tom?" said Windy.

Pavel spoke as if he'd just sucked on a helium balloon, "Yes."

"Pavel," began Jenny, "is an old friend of the family. Our dad phoned ahead and asked him to help us." She knew it was a rubbish lie.

Pavel suddenly became very interested in his feet.

"Oh, I see," said Windy, wistfully. "It's beautiful outside just now. Fancy taking Billy out for a walk around the deck?"

Jenny had to think who Billy was for a few seconds. *Why*

had they lied about their names? "Of course," she blurted.

"We might get lucky and see a minky whale or a manx shearwater. It's June, so we might even catch a glimpse of a killer whale," said Windy.

"Seen all those," said Jenny, nonchalantly.

"What about you...?" She just managed to stop herself from calling him Pavel again. "Are you coming out?"

"Nah," said Pavel, "I'll stay in here with Billy." He drew out the word 'Billy' as if he was talking to a two year old.

"Fine," snapped Jenny.

Outside, the sun was high and Jenny could feel the warm wafts of air produced by the big red and yellow funnel wash over her.

They were well out of the harbour and a gentle roll caused her to steady herself on the newly painted rail.

"So, you've seen orcas?" said Windy.

Jenny knew that an orca was the other name for a killer whale. "Yes, lots of times," she said. "I've seen sperm whales too, and porpoises, and dolphins and..."

"I've never seen an otter," said Windy. His binoculars were already up at his eyes.

"We see otters all the time at Hushwish," said Jenny.

"Hushwish?" asked Windy.

"That's where I live."

"It must be a wonderful place to live," said Windy.

"It is just now," said Jenny, under her breath. The urge to tell Windy everything was overpowering.

"Well, well, well..." said a deep voice.

Jenny looked down the deck and froze.

"The whole Island's looking for you, girl."

It was Jimmy McGovern, the man who took the lambs off

the island of Harris to the markets in Dingwall and sometimes Oban. It must have been his lorry she'd seen in the ferry lane at Lochboisdale.

Windy lowered his binoculars and whispered out of the side of his mouth, "You know him?"

McGovern had been intercepted by a couple of farmers. They'd distracted him for a moment.

Jenny ducked behind Windy. "He's creepy," she said. "Always laughs at his own jokes. Drinks too much."

Windy eyed the big man suspiciously.

She'd always been told by her father to humour McGovern, but she knew that her father hadn't liked the man either. *What am I going to do?*

She tucked her giveaway blonde hair into her hood and suddenly thought of Lord and Pavel. McGovern would recognise them too.

"Hey, wait a minute," shouted McGovern. The two farmers were obviously beginning to annoy him. He stepped in between them and walked towards Jenny.

"Windy, I need to go to the toilet," she said.

"Sure," said Windy, still eyeing McGovern. He opened the heavy door for Jenny and she darted under his arm. She made for the ladies' toilet but ran straight into Pavel and Lord.

"Thank goodness," she panted.

"What's up with you?" said Pavel.

Lord was licking her hand, his tail wagging furiously.

"Hey, come back here!" shouted McGovern.

"I've been spotted," hissed Jenny. "It's all over now."

Pavel pulled her across the inner deck until they reached the door on the port side of the boat. "Quick, through here."

They staggered out into the fresh air on the other side of

the boat.

"It's McGovern," repeated Jenny.

"I know who it is," said Pavel.

They flattened themselves against the big red and yellow funnel.

Pavel edged out a little and craned his neck to look along the deck. "I think he's gone."

Carefully, Jenny stole a glance down the gangway. They edged away from the funnel until they were directly under a set of spars holding a lifeboat.

A sudden gust of wind whipped her long hair over her face.

She felt a tap on the shoulder. "Going somewhere?"

CHAPTER FIFTEEN
FEELING SICK

Jimmy McGovern was a bull of a man. It was hard to tell where his head stopped and his neck began. His shoulders were about three feet in breadth and the rest of his body maintained the same proportions all the way down to his knees. There, a pair of enormous, black wellie boots stole the show.

Jenny stared at his feet. They were huge. She remembered him saying that the rubber factory in Dumfries made his boots to order: a size twenty-two. His hands were like shovels: monstrous, but big and bloated like his nose.

"You're in deep water now, my girl," bellowed McGovern.

Jenny had forgotten how loud he was. She tried to maintain a look of surprise. "I am?"

"Yes," laughed Pavel, "we're in the middle of the sea."

"I'm not talking about that and fine you know it, boy."

Lord barked up at him.

Windy wandered over, his binoculars still swinging from his neck. "Everything all right, Jean?"

"Jean, is it?" scoffed McGovern, never once taking his piggy eyes off her.

"Sometimes I'm called Jean," she whimpered.

She felt as if her whole world was folding in on itself; her stomach certainly was, and the roll of the boat wasn't helping.

"Well, are we going to stand here all day or are we going to go inside and explain ourselves?"

"Explain what?" said Windy.

Pavel rounded on Jenny. "You look a bit peely-wally," he said.

McGovern's shovel of a hand found Pavel's shoulder. "And you'll have a bit of explaining to do as well, laddie."

Windy followed them inside. "Look, what's all this about?"

Windy looked like a stick insect standing next to McGovern.

"And who might you be, sir?" enquired McGovern.

"Me... I..." stuttered Windy, "I'm simply someone who wants Jean and Tom to get down to Oban safely. Their father has a very important interview today."

McGovern's laugh blasted across the canteen, causing several passengers to spill hot tea down their chins. "I never pegged you as a liar, Miss MacLeod," he growled.

Jenny didn't know what to do or say. She felt an overwhelming urge to cry but her stomach was telling her something else. It clenched like a fist inside her. She spied the movement of the horizon through a salt-encrusted window and suddenly felt worse. "I..." She couldn't speak. There wasn't time. She spied the door of the ladies' toilet and bolted.

"Hey, now!" McGovern lunged out at her, but she ducked beneath his scooping hands and made it to the door. Her legs felt like jelly as she staggered inside. She placed both hands on the nearest toilet bowl and heaved. Again and again and again she vomited until her stomach was completely empty. But it didn't stop there; she continued to retch even though there was nothing left to come up.

Shaking and sweating, all she could think of was survival.

* * *

It was 11.30 a.m. at the Murdoch's house and it was completely silent. Mrs Murdoch had spent most of her life alone, cooking or cleaning in preparation for Sandy or Angus coming home for their tea. She had grown used to the silence, built herself a routine of sorts that gave her some sense of purpose. Today, however, that world was far away.

She sat on the piano stool for a while and stared out into the yard. Then, restless, she wandered through to the kitchen and aimlessly opened and shut a few cupboard doors. She didn't know what to do with herself.

The manila envelope lay on the kitchen table, its contents strewn out over the polished pine top. She looked at the huge pile of washing on the kitchen floor and just sighed. She saw the dishes to be done in the sink and couldn't face them. *How could Angus do such a thing? Had she never really known him?* He'd been keeping letters back from the MacLeods.

"Wait!" she yelled. A vision of her husband, Angus, rummaging round in the piano stool jumped into her head. She ran through to the piano then opened the lid of the piano stool. Just music and...Then she saw it; a piece of wood protruding from the side of the stool. She flicked it out further with her nails and then caught hold of the corner of a small drawer. She could hardly get it to open, it was so stuffed full of letters. A big bundle of brown manila letters that all looked exactly like the one lying on her kitchen table. And they'd all been opened. She pulled one free of the pile and read it. Her mouth fell open. She didn't know what to do.

The phone purred into life.

She jumped up and knocked the receiver off the hook. It bounced on its curly wire like a puppet until her fingers found it and fumbled it back into her hand.

"Yes?" she answered.

"Any sign of her?"

It was Angus. She froze, unsure what to say.

"Are you still there?" pressed Angus.

"She's not here," she said. Her voice was monotone.

There was a pause.

"We checked Hushwish and the ferry terminal," said Angus.

"Good," she said simply.

There was another pause.

"Ellen, are you all right?"

Her heart raced as she stared at the envelope. *Two hundred and two thousand pounds,* she thought. *How could he keep that kind of news from them?* "I'm all right. How are you feeling?"

"How am I feeling?" repeated Angus. "Look, we've contacted the police and they've called the boat. It was diverted to Lochmaddy. They've looked on board but no sign of her or Pavel."

"So, where is she?" asked Ellen.

"I don't know. The police even checked with the ferry staff at Lochmaddy. No sign of her there either."

Should she confront Angus about the MacLeods' letter? "Angus...?"

"Need to go," he snapped. "McGovern's phoning me."

The line went dead.

McGovern, thought Ellen. He was a big oaf. *Is he involved? Does Sandy know about the letters?*

Ellen Murdoch could tell that her husband was at his

wit's end. The more she thought about Jenny MacLeod and her father, Hamish, the more she felt the knot grow inside her. It was a feeling she'd never experienced before. It was a wretched mix of betrayal, mistrust and anger. Most of all it was anger.

She spied the car keys on the hook behind the back door and decided there and then to go and look for Jenny herself. She'd forgotten to ask where Angus had been calling from. He'd said that he was going to Glasgow. Hamish MacLeod was in Glasgow.

She pulled on her coat and picked up her handbag. She didn't have the whole story but she knew that Angus was up to no good, and he had Sandy in tow. She was going to get the whole story one way or another.

She opened the front door and gasped with fright.

Pavel's father was standing on her front step.

"Are you going to find Jenny, Mrs Murdoch?" he asked.

Ellen looked into his grey eyes and said, "...Yes."

"I'd like to come with you, please," he said.

"Fine." She skirted round the little man and opened the door of her Volkswagen Polo. "Well, don't just stand there, Bernard. Jump in."

"Where are we going?" said Bernard.

"Glasgow," said Ellen, never more sure in her whole life that she was doing the right thing.

CHAPTER SIXTEEN
THE BIG CLUE

A lady with a couple of toddlers in tow opened Jenny's cubicle door. "Are you okay?" she asked.

"Not so good," whimpered Jenny.

"Do you want some sea-sickness tablets?" asked the lady.

Jenny knew it was wrong to take sweets from a stranger, never mind drugs. "Yes, please." Her face was still wet with tears.

The toddlers began tussling in the doorway as the lady opened her handbag and searched inside. "Here they are," she said, offering Jenny a tiny pink pill. "Just place it on your tongue and... Oh... what age are you?"

"I'm ten," said Jenny.

"Ten, ten..." muttered the lady. She read the small print on the back of the light blue pack. "That's fine. Just put it on your tongue and it will melt."

Jenny stuck out her tongue and watched as the toddlers stuck theirs out right back at her. She shivered as the tablet dissolved. Thoughts of Windy, Pavel and, most of all, McGovern, were beginning to seep back into her mind. Jenny pulled herself up using the handle on the cistern and slumped back onto the toilet seat.

"Who's the big man waiting for you outside in the gangway?" asked the woman. "Your dad?"

"No..." Jenny sensed the lady's concern and decided to make the most of it. Her stomach had stopped cramping. "He's my uncle," she lied. *That was lie number ten, or something*, she thought. *So I may as well keep going.* "He's always hitting us and..." Totally drained, it was easy for Jenny to cry, so she let the tears pour free.

"But he's a brute of a man," gasped the woman.

She pulled her wriggling boys in close and eyed the door that led to the gangway with suspicion.

"My dad has warned him to leave us alone but..."

"I've heard enough. Just you wait there a minute."

Jenny watched as the woman produced a mobile from her bag. "I'm going to call someone," she said.

Jenny wondered who. "The tall, skinny boy is my adopted brother, and that's my dog out there too."

The woman showed her the palm of her hand, as if to shush her, and then dialled a long number.

"Oh," said Jenny, suddenly remembering Windy, "the other man... the one with the fleecy jacket and the wispy hair, he's a nice man who..." she managed to add a few deep sobs into the mix, "tried to help us."

"Michael," said the woman, "it's Ruth here. There's a small girl on the ferry who's terrified. It's her uncle. He seems to be out of control." The woman cupped the phone and whispered, "I'd say he was the violent type." The woman smiled reassuringly at Jenny and then nodded as the other person on the phone chattered. Her toddlers had unravelled a toilet roll all over the wet floor. They were yelping with glee.

The woman tried to catch one of their flaying arms but they giggled and ducked out of her reach.

"Yes," said the woman, now very distracted. "And you'll bring the police? ...Excellent!" She snapped the mobile shut and eyed the closed door. "I'll go first. Don't worry about a thing."

"Be careful," warned Jenny. "He drinks a lot, but it doesn't stop him driving his big truck. I'm so frightened he'll make us go with him."

The woman flicked her phone open and updated Michael.

Jenny took a deep breath as the door swung open.

* * *

Outside in the gangway, Windy struggled with Lord. The dog had taken an intense dislike to the big man called McGovern.

Pavel thought he'd heard the ladies' toilet door open at last.

McGovern stepped back to let a lady with two toddlers come out into the gangway. Strangely, the woman glared at him in the most hostile way before dragging her children away.

McGovern removed his cap in deference to the lady and smiled. The woman, however, answered the chivalrous gesture with a verbal attack of Herculean proportions.

"You're not fit to have children under your care!" she finished.

McGovern flinched and flushed bright red.

"But..."

"But, nothing. You're a bully and a brute."

"I'm what?" McGovern protested.

Jenny popped her head out of the toilet door. The woman

took Jenny's hand. "If you so much as lay a hand on this young girl, I'll have you and your truck thrown off the ship."

Pavel wondered who this woman was? To have such power...

Jenny looked awful, haggard and gaunt. She stared up at McGovern and quailed. In a shaky voice, she whimpered, "Don't hit us any more."

Pavel felt his chest expand with pride. She was learning. His student was learning. He had guided her on the true path.

* * *

The island of Mull soon loomed large on their starboard side as they neared Oban. They'd spent three hours beside the purser's office with no sign of McGovern. It was clear that he'd retreated to the bar for the duration.

Thanks to Lord's incessant barking, Windy hadn't heard a word McGovern had said.

"Sea sickness is a curse," said Windy, staring at Jenny.

"I feel much better now," said Jenny. The tablets the woman had given her had stopped the horrible feeling of nausea. Pavel had even complimented her on her ingenuity. "You're a natural," he'd said.

"Fancy a bit of fresh air?" said Windy.

Jenny glimpsed a castle on her right, through the porthole in the door.

"Come on," said Pavel. He led them to the opposite door. They all stepped outside and held onto the rail. The water was much calmer now.

"What's that?" Jenny pointed to a huge church with two towers.

"That's the cathedral," said Windy.

"And that?" said Jenny. Her heart was racing.

Above the town, on the brow of a steep hill, she could see a circular building that looked a bit like the pictures she'd seen of the Colosseum in Rome.

"That structure is supposed to be a folly," said Windy.

"What's a folly?" asked Pavel.

Lord looked up at Windy expectantly.

"A folly is a building built for fun. It's supposed to look impressive, stand out."

"Why put all that energy into building something like that?" said Pavel.

Windy shrugged. "It would make a great site for a wind farm." He licked his fingers and tested the wind direction. "The WPD is perfect."

Ignoring Windy's words, Jenny caught Pavel's arm and heaved him further up the rail. She pointed at a dark building next to the harbour. "That's it. It's the name of dad's hospital. It's the girl's name that I couldn't remember!"

Pavel looked confused for a moment. He staggered after her, following her gaze.

"What girl's name?" said Windy, catching them up.

"Alexandra," said Jenny, her heart pounding even faster.

CHAPTER SEVENTEEN
THE BOOKSHOP

"Now, you're sure your father said it was okay to give you a lift?" asked Windy.

"I gave him your registration," Pavel lied. "Besides, it's only for a few yards," he added.

Rolling off the ferry in Windy's car, Jenny and Pavel could barely contain their laughter. McGovern was being frogmarched off the ferry to a waiting police car. His big red face looked about to explode and his arms were flailing wildly in protest. His tweed hat spun off his head as a further two policemen tried to restrain him. It briefly jiggled in the wind and then spun down into the gap between the boat and the harbour wall like a frisbee.

Jenny caught Windy's smile in the rear view mirror.

"You said you knew him?" said Windy.

"Poor man. Not quite the full shilling, I'm afraid," said Pavel.

Jenny was bent double and very close to wetting herself.

Lord gave a final snarl and then began licking Jenny's face.

"Where is your father?" said Windy.

"Still at his interview, I would think," said Pavel, still

chuckling and pretending to examine his watch. "He said he would meet us at the railway station. Could you drop us there?"

"Of course," said Windy.

They drove out of the ferry terminal, swinging left up an incline before tipping down past a library on their right. Jenny could see a roundabout ahead.

"Now, have you got your purse this time?" Jenny checked her duffel bag as Windy veered left into the railway car park.

Pavel suddenly caught hold of Jenny's arm.

Still giggling to herself, she whispered, "What is it?"

Pavel stared straight ahead and asked, "Is there an airport near Oban?"

Windy's eyes looked at them in the mirror. "A small one."

Pavel jerked Jenny's sleeve and nodded ahead.

"It's Murdoch," he whispered urgently, his long face drained of all colour.

"It can't be," hissed Jenny.

Pavel whispered sharply into her ear, "It is!"

As Windy drove closer, Jenny saw the unmistakable figure of Angus Murdoch standing beside the waiting room door. He had several men with him whom she vaguely recognised and someone else they both knew very well. She took in a breath. "Sandy's here too?"

"Everything all right?" Windy enquired.

"Yes," she lied, again.

Pavel leaned forward. "We were just thinking that it would be good to buy our father a book. Get him a present..."

"To celebrate his interview," said Jenny, instantly realising that it was a stupid thing to have said.

Windy chuckled to himself. "I've never heard of an interview present."

"He loves books," added Pavel.

Mr Murdoch was scanning every single passenger who walked from the ferry to the station.

"He's not looking for us in a car," whispered Pavel.

"He looks pretty upset," said Jenny.

"Yeah, well, he probably saw McGovern, his snitch, being bundled into the police car."

Windy spun the car round and turned another corner.

"There!" said Jenny.

"Waterstone's," said Windy. "What kind of books does he like?"

There was a short, uncomfortable silence before Pavel blurted out, "Fantasy and adventure books."

Jenny stared at him.

Pavel just shrugged his shoulders.

As they pulled up to the impressive façade of the bookshop, Jenny and Pavel said their goodbyes to Windy. Jenny hauled out her duffel bag while Pavel turned to catch Lord's lead.

"Look," said Windy, "I can't really stop here and you won't be able to take Billy in there, so why don't I drive round the block a few times. Give you a few minutes to choose a book. You can take Billy back then."

Jenny knew that they didn't really have a choice. Pavel nodded. "Sounds good." He closed the side door of the car. Lord began barking as Windy pulled away.

"Now what?" said Jenny, looking over Pavel's shoulder for any sign of the Murdochs or their henchmen.

Pavel caught her hand. "In here, Jenny."

They opened the glass door and walked into the big bookshop. It stretched back for what seemed like a hundred yards, row upon row of books on either side. Jenny closed her eyes for a moment and took a deep breath. "I love the smell of bookshops," she said.

"You've never been in one before, Jenny," said Pavel.

"I still love the smell."

Pavel grinned. "So do I. Let's move further in. Head for the back of the shop."

Several men and women wearing black shirts busied themselves, stacking shelves and chatting to customers.

As they neared the back of the shop Jenny felt Pavel grip her wrist tightly and jerk her down behind a high shelf.

"I'm sure I just saw Sandy," he said.

"What?" gasped Jenny. "He hates books."

"Which means that he's in here looking for us," said Pavel.

Staring at the cover of a book called The Magic Scales her mind raced. She still hadn't spoken to her father. It was now a full day since they'd confronted the wind farm protestors. Pavel moved further round the display and she followed, still bent double. Sandy Murdoch's voice was very close by. He was asking one of the bookstore staff if he'd seen a small girl with long blonde hair and a lanky boy, a bit older.

Pavel pulled her round the display and in behind a pillar.

"I think so," said the man. "I just saw a couple of kids like that near the Scottish Author section."

Sandy shouted to someone. "Cover the door and tell my dad."

Jenny began to shake but Pavel moved them on again. They edged round two more displays and passed a set of stairs on their right. Pavel caught her eye and whispered. "Let's go up."

"What?" protested Jenny. "They'll see us."

Pavel grabbed a heavy book on cooking and lobbed it as far

as he could across the shop.

Jenny's heart sank. There was a big bang as it toppled a row of books on the other side of the shop. As soon as the commotion began, Pavel pulled her forward. She raced up the stairs and through a glass door marked 'private'.

They both waited, listening.

She could hear the shouts of men downstairs in the shop but, so far, no one had followed them.

"Your distraction must have worked," she whispered.

"Perhaps," said Pavel. "Now to get out of here."

Upstairs in the warm room, books sat in piles between coffee cups and sheets of paper.

"Lost, are we?" said a voice.

Feet were thumping up the stairs.

CHAPTER EIGHTEEN
THE BATTLE
ON THE BRAE

An older man with an inquisitive expression had appeared from behind a pile of books. He crossed the floor in a matter of seconds and snibbed the door shut behind them just as Sandy Murdoch's big, ruddy face appeared at the glass. He waved his finger at Sandy and pointed to the sign marked 'private'.

Sandy peered over the older man's shoulder but Jenny and Pavel had ducked down well out of sight. They could just see Sandy through a half-inch crack between the top of a pile books and the bottom of the wooden table.

Sandy wavered for a moment, trying the handle while leering at the older man. Then, with one final glance round their room, the school bully edged away from the glass door and rattled down the steps.

"A friend of yours?" asked the man.

"Not exactly," said Jenny.

"He's the school bully," said Pavel, for once telling the truth.

"A nasty piece of work by the looks of him," said the man.

He lifted the receiver of a buff-coloured phone and dialled one number. "Jimmy? The big idiot wearing the donkey jacket... yes, I know. A bit of a thug." The older man nodded. "Chuck them all out."

Jenny felt her heart lift.

"After that, come up here. I have a couple of stowaways." The older man smiled and then invited Pavel and Jenny to sit down. His round glasses glinted in the strip lights above their heads.

They hesitated for a moment and then sat down sheepishly between another two piles of books on a wooden bench.

"So you just came in to hide?" he asked.

"Not really," said Jenny.

"We came in for a book," said Pavel.

"What kind of book?" asked the man.

"It's for my father," said Jenny. When she lied this time, she tried to picture her own father, not the imaginary father they'd told Windy about. She hoped the self-deception would cancel out the untruth.

"What kind of book does he like to read?"

Now Jenny was confused. Pavel had told Windy that her imaginary father liked fantasy, so she thought she'd stick to that. "He's a farmer, but he likes fantasy stuff..."

"Something with a message," added Pavel.

"A fable, perhaps," said the man, thoughtfully. He shuffled a few things on the table and dug out a book with a white cover. It had a painting of a sheep's head on the front, only it was in two halves: one half black-faced the other half white-faced. The sheep's eye's looked mean. "Pure Wool," said the man. He turned the book over in his hands. "A modern fable. How's that?" He handed it to Jenny just as another man, much younger, opened the glass door marked 'private'.

"My dad likes sheep," said Jenny.

"How much is it?" asked Pavel, producing a couple of coins.

"You can have it. Let's call it a sample," said the older man.

Jenny thought this was very nice of him. She took it and placed it in her duffel bag.

"On you go," said the other man. "The coast is clear."

Jenny thought he sounded like Pavel.

Not just the silly saying, but his accent too.

Pavel hesitated.

"And there's a man with a dog in the backseat of his car double parked at the front of the shop. Says he's waiting on a Tom and a Jean. I take it he's not after you as well?"

"No, he's a friend," said Jenny. She got up and thanked the older man. Pavel did too.

"Dzhehnkcooyeh," Pavel said as he passed the younger man.

The younger man smiled and ushered them downstairs.

"I heard you talking earlier," he said to Pavel, "thought we might have something in common."

"You're both from Poland?" asked Jenny.

Pavel smiled at Jenny then shook the young man's hand before edging out of the glass doors. Jenny glanced up and down the street for any sign of the Murdochs. The young man followed them out and saw them safely into Windy's car.

"Hi, you two!" It was Windy, and in seconds they were in the back seat with Lord. They waved to the young Polish bookseller and pulled away.

Jenny soon spotted Sandy and his thugs walking along the strand and slumped down in her seat.

"Get your book?" asked Windy.

"Yeah, thanks," said Pavel.

Lord was wagging his tail hard. It kept whipping Jenny's face as she pulled on his collar. She was worried that Sandy would recognise him.

Jenny produced the book and showed it to Windy in the rear-view mirror.

Pavel jabbed her in the ribs and pointed up to a steep road. "We'll head up there after Windy takes us back to the station."

Windy turned right and then right again, eventually reaching the roundabout at the station. Jenny prayed there'd be no sign of the Murdochs.

To her relief, there wasn't.

"Just here's fine," said Pavel, still scanning the station.

"Look," said Windy. "Take this." He handed Jenny a piece of paper. "It's my mobile number. If you have any trouble with anything at all, give me a call."

"Thanks," said Jenny. She nudged Pavel.

"Dzhehnkcooyeh," said Pavel.

A quizzical look on his face, Windy waved them both goodbye.

"We never really explained how we could be brother and sister with such different accents," said Jenny.

"He was too polite to ask," said Pavel.

They walked round the edge of the station and on past the bookshop until they reached a side road that climbed towards the folly that looked like the Colosseum.

Panting, Jenny asked, "Do you still think Windy's the enemy?"

Pavel didn't answer. Instead he stopped and busied himself counting the remains of his money. "I've got one pound fifty. How much have you got?"

Still annoyed at Pavel's mistrust of Windy, just because he

helped build wind farms, Jenny spun the duffel bag off her shoulder and pulled her purse out of the top pocket. She popped it open and pulled out the notes.

Lord growled.

A big freckled hand caught her wrist. "I'll take that."

Jenny screamed.

Sandy Murdoch's horrible grinning face was only inches from hers.

Pavel struggled with two other boys.

"Help!" yelled Jenny. The road was quiet. Jenny made to shout out again, but Sandy put his hand over her mouth.

Lord bit down on Sandy's wrist and he screamed out. "Argh! You stupid mutt." He tried to punch Lord, letting go of his grip on Jenny.

Lord bit him again and this time Sandy backed off, blood running down his wrist and over the cuff of his shirt.

The two other boys pulled Pavel back. Lord snapped at them.

Sandy picked up a big stone from the side of an overflowing skip and launched it at Lord.

It missed but caught one of Pavel's attackers on the shin.

"Argh! Ya dunderheed!" he roared.

Jenny recognised him as one of Sandy's older pals from Stornoway.

She swung her duffel bag and hit Sandy Murdoch between his legs.

He crumpled, still nursing his bleeding hand. Pavel smacked one of the boys on the cheek and broke free.

In seconds they were tearing back down the hill towards the town centre, Lord yelping behind them.

Pavel spun round and caught hold of Lord's trailing lead.

As he turned back, however, he smacked straight into a giant.

Winded, he fell back.

Jenny tried to duck round but came face to face with Angus Murdoch.

Lord began barking again.

"Quiet, dug!" yelled McGovern. Lord cowered.

Mr Murdoch took her bag. "McGovern would have been locked up if I hadn't stepped in." He pushed Jenny across to the ruddy-faced McGovern who held her tight beside Pavel. Mr Murdoch rummaged for a few seconds and then pulled a manila envelope free of her jumbled up clothes. "So, Jenny, you found the letters?"

CHAPTER NINETEEN
THE MART

Sandy Murdoch and McGovern rounded on Pavel and Jenny. Lord had been tied to the metal railings of a circular ring. There was sawdust on the floor.

They'd been taken to an auction mart a few miles south of Oban.

"There won't be anybody here until the morning," hissed Sandy.

"So you needn't try and shout for help; no one will hear you," added McGovern. His big broad shadow trailed behind him as he turned and moved towards her duffel bag. "It's getting cold in here, Sandy."

Sandy Murdoch laughed and kicked the bag into the middle of the ring. "Do you think it will burn, Mr McGovern?"

"What, with all these books in it? Aye, son, like dry heather."

Sandy tipped it upside down and began shaking it until all its contents spilled onto the floor.

A single bulb lit the empty auction hall. Sandy kicked Jenny's clothes and books into a pile and chucked several handfuls of straw on top before striking a match. He produced the manila envelope from the inside of his donkey jacket and grinned maniacally. "Your poor dad will never get a chance to sign this now." He dropped a match onto the straw and moved back towards Jenny and Pavel. They'd been tied together with orange bailer twine. He grabbed Jenny's chin and waved the letter in front of her eyes. "Shame, really. Old Hamish might not even make it through the night. Fighting for his life, I'm told."

"Liar!" screamed Jenny, pulling away from his dirty fingers.

Pavel tried to kick Sandy, but Sandy skipped over Pavel's swinging leg and slapped his face.

Pavel slumped against the rails of the auction mart, pulling Jenny onto her back.

Sandy waved the letter at her face and laughed again.

McGovern cracked open a can of beer and handed it to Sandy. "We may as well make ourselves comfortable, boy."

Sandy took a swig and let the froth run down his chin. He coughed and then wiped his face with the sleeve of his jacket. He took one last look at the letter before throwing it at the fire. "By tomorrow, your dad will be dead and my dad will be rich."

"No he won't," yelled Jenny. She fought off the urge to cry. She wouldn't show any signs of weakness, not in front of him.

Behind Sandy, her duffel bag was ablaze. It reminded her of the burning effigy of the windmill on Hushwish Bay. Suddenly, something inside her clicked. "Pavel," she whispered.

"What is it, Jenny?" he whispered back. His mouth was full of blood.

"Look away. The fire is going to explode any minute."

"What?" gasped Pavel.

"There's a tin of flea spray in there and..."

"Flea spray?" said Pavel.

"For Lord, and some perfume and..."

Pavel rolled further away from the centre of the auction ring, dragging Jenny with him.

Sandy and McGovern were standing right next to the fire, laughing and swigging beer.

BANG!

The blue flash of light that caught Sandy and McGovern took them by surprise. McGovern flew back towards the railings of the auction ring while Sandy was thrown roughly onto the concrete floor next to Lord.

Jenny had felt the heat on the back of her neck.

Sandy screamed as he tried to put out the flames on his trousers. McGovern, on the other hand, lay very still, smoke seeping upwards from his heavy jacket.

"Are you okay, Jenny?" said Pavel.

Jenny rolled and twisted until her back was against Pavel's again. "Yes, I think so."

Lord snapped at Sandy.

"Get back!" Sandy whimpered, still swatting his smoking legs.

"Look, Pavel," said Jenny, "The podium's caught fire!"

The wooden platform where the auctioneer normally stood had begun to crackle and spark.

"It will spread to the seats and the roof," said Pavel, struggling to break free of the orange twine that bound him.

Jenny felt the hard, nylon twine cut into her. "Stop it, Pavel. It's hurting me."

The heat intensified.

She turned her face away as another explosion burst out from the fire.

"There'll be all sorts of things in here that could go up," said Pavel, twisting again.

"Stop it!" shouted Jenny. The pain in her wrists was agonising.

Sandy had moved over to McGovern, who was out cold. The flames grew higher and Sandy heaved at the big man. McGovern's huge feet were dangerously close to the flames.

"Undo our ropes and we'll help you!" shouted Pavel.

Sandy glared at them for a moment and then pulled at McGovern's coat again. The big man barely moved an inch.

"Untie us!" shouted Jenny.

Another bang forced Sandy back from the prostrate McGovern.

Lord was barking incessantly.

Jenny was coughing. The smoke was as black as pitch and thickening by the second. "Sandy!" she shouted.

"He's a coward," said Pavel.

Sandy wavered above McGovern for a second and then bolted out of the ring.

"Sandy!" screamed Jenny.

"Shuffle back from the flames," said Pavel.

"I can't," said Jenny. Her eyes stung so much that she had to close them tight.

"Stay low," urged Pavel. "Keep your face next to the concrete."

Jenny felt the warm concrete against her cheek.

"How could he just leave us to..."

"Help me, then!" It was Sandy. He was cutting their ropes.

Jenny pulled herself free of Pavel and the rails and leapt over to where Lord was barking. She felt the dog's warm coat and pushed her face against his muzzle. "Come on, boy." She traced his lead until she felt the knot on the hot rail. With a grunt of effort, she undid the knot and slid the lead free of the rail. "Come, Lord!" She ran blindly, hitting the rails twice before finding the gap. She ran out into the cold, out of the smoke and horrible heat before falling onto her knees. "Argh!" Her knees jarred off the shale and the pain heightened her senses.

She forced her stinging eyes open and looked round for Pavel. "Pavel!" Her voice was thin against the backdrop of crackling flames and falling timbers. The mart was ablaze.

"Jenny!"

Pavel had helped pull McGovern free of the flames. He was staggering over the car park towards her. His face was black with smoke. "Jenny, now's our chance."

She looked behind him and saw Sandy kneeling over McGovern. The school bully had a mobile pressed to his ear.

"It's now or never," said Pavel.

"Let's go!" shouted Jenny.

CHAPTER TWENTY
THE TRUCK

In the pitch dark of the open field the only light was from the blaze in the distance. Sirens filled the air and high-pitched shouts echoed over the hills behind them.

"Are we safe now?" asked Jenny. She pulled on Lord's lead. He was growling at the sheep that scattered around them.

"We're about a mile away from the mart," said Pavel. "They'll be busy enough." Pavel shushed her. "Wait." He stopped. "Down there." He pointed down the hill.

"What's down there?" asked Jenny.

"The road to Glasgow," said Pavel.

"We can still make it then?"

"Of course we can," said Pavel. "We have to stop the Murdochs building those windmills on your farm."

"But the letter. We left it..." Jenny felt something cold and smooth being placed in her hand.

"Picked it up just in time," said Pavel. "It had fluttered into the corner. Sandy's a rubbish shot. Now, let's get down to that road and hitch a lift."

"We could phone Windy," said Jenny. "Just tell him everything."

"What? You want to tell him that we're trying to stop his wind farm going ahead? Then you want to ask him for a lift to Glasgow? It's a hundred miles away."

"Is that all you're worried about?" said Jenny. She tucked the letter under her coat.

"What?" said Pavel, moving off.

She shouted after him, "Your bloomin' windmills."

Pavel stumbled on a tussock of grass. "No!" he shouted back.

"I just want to get to my dad," said Jenny. "I just want to know he's all right. That's all I'm interested in now." She pulled the letter from her coat and threw it into the darkness.

"Don't be so bloomin' stupid!" shouted Pavel.

He doubled back and checked the ground around her feet. "If you've..."

"If I've what, you'll do what?" Jenny felt her face flush with rage.

Pavel stooped low and picked the letter from the dirt. He took a deep breath. "I want your dad to be safe too. I like your dad. I like you. Most of the time," he added. He brushed a clump of mud off the letter and shook it. "But why throw away your mum's money? She left you this so you and your dad wouldn't have to worry. So you could live on the farm the way you always have."

"I know," said Jenny, "with no windmills." She tugged the letter back from Pavel and put it in her inside pocket.

She could hear the road. The rumble of cars grew louder as they walked further down the boggy field. They found a barbed-wire fence that wobbled precariously as they clambered over.

"There's a lay-by," said Pavel.

Jenny strained to see the outline of a big wagon. "It's

parked up for the night."

"It's the same one we were on," said Jenny. She recognised the triangular bulge of the timber-frame house under its canvas cover.

Pavel crept closer, ducking behind the wagon as a car sped by.

Jenny saw Pavel's laces hanging down from the canvas. "The driver didn't spot your door, then?"

"I told you it was worth tidying up." Pavel quickly undid the laces that kept the canvas together and they climbed inside. He settled Lord down on top of an old sack and led Jenny to the back of the driver's cabin. "He's on his mobile. Listen."

The driver's muffled words drifted back from the cabin: "It's not my fault that it was the wrong kit. Anyway, I don't care. I'm still getting paid either way."

There was a pause.

"Dumbarton at eleven? I'll be there well before that."

Jenny shrugged. What did the driver mean? Pavel pressed his ear against the cabin. "Dumbarton," Pavel whispered.

Jenny shrugged her shoulders again.

"The cat is in the bag," said Pavel, a wry grin forming on his face.

"The cat is what?" Jenny tugged him back from the cabin. "What's that supposed to mean?"

Pavel followed her back into the tangle of wooden struts.

"We have our lift to Glasgow. Well, almost Glasgow."

"Where's Dumbarton?" asked Jenny.

"It's near Loch Lomond but..." Pavel sighed and stretched out on another crumpled hemp sack beside Lord. He placed his hands behind his head and stared up into the darkness of their temporary tent. "It's where my mother lives."

"Your mother?" Jenny had never heard Pavel mention his mum. "So, let me see. Your mum and dad came here from Poland and then split up?"

"Almost," said Pavel. "My mother is English. She's my stepmother, really."

"So your real mother is..."

"I can't even remember her." In the dim light Pavel's face hardened.

"I'm sorry." Jenny found a spot next to Lord.

"My father came to Scotland for a fresh start. He met a nice lady and they settled near Dumbarton. That's where I went to school."

"I thought you said you were in Glasgow?" said Jenny.

"It's near enough. However, my mother and father grew apart. My father wanted to get back to his roots in farming and mum... well, mum has other interests."

"So they split?"

Pavel sighed. "They never divorced, but yes, they split."

"You must get sad sometimes," said Jenny.

"No point crying over spilt milk."

Jenny saw Pavel smile.

"There might be," said Jenny. "You know, if you were on a desert island and the orly thing you'd found to eat or drink in a whole week was a glass of milk, and then it spilled over..."

They both laughed.

Jenny cuddled into _ord. "Do you think McGovern is all right?"

"He was still breathing," said Pavel. "Anyway, I think Sandy will be feeling a lot worse than McGovern. I mean, he let us escape and burnt the mart down into the bargain. His dad will be furious."

"Where does all this leave you?" asked Jenny. "I mean, your father works for Murdoch and..."

"I don't care about all that."

"But your dad's job?"

"Never mind that; where does it leave Murdoch?" said Pavel. "What was he going to do with us? Keep us tied up until the time ran out on the wind farm deal, and then what?"

Jenny hadn't really thought it through until now.

"So you think he was going to hurt us?"

"You can't just go round tying kids up," said Pavel. "If he'd taken it that far..."

"Stop it. I don't want to think about it."

There was a long silence before Pavel asked, "Do you miss your mother?"

Jenny waited until her heart had stopped thumping so hard. "Yes, every day." She sighed and turned to face Pavel. "And don't say anything about spilt milk."

"I would never say anything like that concerning your mum," he said.

"I know," said Jenny. She felt her eyes becoming heavy. Her body ached for sleep. Lord had begun to snore. It reminded her of her dad and she smiled to herself. She had the letter, she was unhurt, and she would be in Glasgow the next day.

"Goodnight, Jenny," said Pavel.

"Good night, and thanks for looking out for me."

"No probs... see you in the morning."

Before long it wasn't just Lord that was snoring.

CHAPTER TWENTY-ONE
DUMBARTON ROCK

Jenny woke with a jolt. Disorientated, she knelt up on all fours and tried to remember where she was. "Lord," she whispered, giving the old dog a big hug.

Lord answered by giving her face a wash with his long, wet tongue.

Jenny wiped away the crool with her sleeve and then gave Pavel a shake. "Pavel? Where are we? Wake up!"

Pavel grunted and then pulled himself to his feet. "We've stopped."

"I know that," said Jenny. "But where have we stopped? Come on, Pavel."

"All right, all right," moaned Pavel. "Keep your hair on." He rubbed his eyes and found the cut he'd made in the canvas the day before at Lochboisdale.

Jenny and Lord crept up behind him.

"I can't see anything from here," moaned Pavel.

He spun round and looked up at the roof. The canvas was stretched over the wooden kit house. "There is a hole in the cover. I can see daylight through it." He scrambled up the wooden trusses and found his lamb's-foot knife.

"Pavel!" hissed Jenny. "Don't..."

"Oops," said Pavel. "Too late." He'd cut another criss-cross in the canvas. He popped his head out into the morning air.

Jenny leapt up to join him.

"It's Dumbarton all right," he said. "Look!" He pointed to a massive lump of granite, roughly the same shape as a pair of camel's humps. There was a castle perched between the twin peaks. "That's Dumbarton Rock," said Pavel.

Jenny felt the cool breeze on her cheeks. "It's amazing." Apart from the castle, she could see that they were next to a big corrugated building on the side of a small river that seemed to lead into a bigger one.

"We're down at the boat house," said Pavel. He climbed down through the tangle of wooden spars. "The driver must be sleeping."

Sliding down from the side of the truck, they edged away and walked across a park to some playing fields and what looked like a running track, all pegged out with rope and ribbons.

"It must be the cross country race today," said Pavel. "I came second here in Primary Six."

Jenny watched Lord run after a few crows. These crows were completely black, different from the grey, hooded ones in Harris. The old, rough-looking sheepdog looked out of place on the well-mown lawn. It was as alien a world to Lord as it was to her. She wandered over to a railing that overlooked the bigger of the two rivers.

Pavel eased in beside her. "All you have to do is follow that river, and turn right at the Erskine Bridge and we'll be at the Royal Alexandra Hospital." Then Pavel pointed up at Dumbarton Rock. "That castle up there sits on the boundary between the River Leven and the big river, the Clyde. The Clyde flows out to the sea from here. Can you see how it gets wider the further north you look?" He leaned out over the rail and pointed up at the distant mountains.

"So how do we get to the hospital?" asked Jenny.

"The Royal Alexandra Hospital," corrected Pavel. He looked back down at the River Leven, with its boats and buoys. "Well, we've no money so..."

"What are you thinking, Pavel?" asked Jenny.

"I'm thinking that there's only one real road leading from here to the Erskine Bridge. The Murdochs might wait for us at Milton or they might go straight to the hospital. I'm thinking that they'll never look for us on a boat."

"Look, Pavel, I don't want to have made it this far just to drown in one of those rickety boats." Jenny pointed back at the River Leven.

"It must be well before six in the morning," Pavel mused.

"How do you know that?" asked Jenny.

Pavel smiled and Jenny looked behind her. A large clock face on a grey church tower showed that it was a quarter to six. By the time she'd turned round, however, Pavel was gone. Lord had scampered off too. She saw Lord disappear down a ramp. "Wait!" she shouted. Jenny ran after them, but by the time she'd caught them up, they were already walking down a slope towards a small harbour. Pavel jumped onto one of the boats. She looked about nervously for any sign of a security guard or even the truck driver, but there was no one else.

Pavel waved at her.

"We shouldn't..." she began, but Pavel just waved more vigorously.

"Come on. They're not all rickety," he said.

Jenny ran down the incline and almost tripped on a thick rope.

"Jenny McLeod," announced Pavel, "your luxury cruiser awaits."

"This is stealing," she hissed. She stared wildly about her before jumping on board. On the deck, Lord wagged his tail and nuzzled in. "But the doors are locked and the boat's tied up."

Pavel just shook his head and produced his trusty lamb's-foot knife. "Both problems can be sorted with this." He began working on the thick rope. "You know, I'm not proud of these skills. I just got in with a bad crowd when I lived down here. A right bad crowd."

"You mean that bully you talked about, who was even worse than Sandy?"

"He was one of them. Yes." The rope frayed and then separated allowing Pavel to cut through the individual strands. "I told you he was called Flynn?"

"Yes, but..." Jenny stared about her, convinced they were going to be arrested on the spot.

"Well, he was evil but smart with it, and that's the wrong kind of mix. A real bad..."

"Apple," finished Jenny. "You see, I know some of your stupid sayings too." She felt her heart scrunch up inside her chest as the boat began to drift out into the river.

Pavel worked on the lock of the cabin. "You know, if I can't get this lock picked in about one minute we'll probably hit that old boat out there."

"Brilliant!" snapped Jenny. Lord punctuated her outburst with a sharp woof.

"Don't panic, don't panic." Pavel wiggled his knife a little faster in the lock and it clicked. "There!" The cruiser was picking up speed.

"Quick," urged Pavel. "Get inside."

Jenny wobbled as she stepped into the cabin.

"It's just the tide," said Pavel. "Lucky for us, it's pulling us out into the Clyde. Now where's the ignition?" Pavel randomly flicked switches and turned dials until he found a tiny brass key. "Got it!"

They were only feet from the old boat that was moored mid-stream.

The engine puttered into life. Pavel pushed the throttle forward and turned the wheel. "It's going to be close."

Jenny held on tight as the cruiser veered recklessly.

Bang!

The cruiser shuddered, knocking Jenny backwards. "You've hit it!" she yelled.

"She's going to need a bit of paint work after that," said Pavel.

Jenny noticed the sweat on his forehead.

"Where are we going?" said Jenny.

"Out there," said Pavel, frantically turning the wheel.

Jenny saw the wide expanse of the Clyde looming ahead of them, the huge outcrop of Dumbarton Rock on their left.

"Why don't you go below and see what you can find?" said Pavel. "I need to concentrate."

"Fine," said Jenny, still unsteady on her feet. She climbed through a brown door and down a set of polished steps. Her hand moved up and down a smooth Formica wall until her fingers found the light switch. There was a kitchen, every bit as posh as the Murdochs', and a fancy door that led to a bedroom. She peered inside the bedroom and saw a mirror with all sorts of perfumes and potions spilt over the sink. Pavel's antics above must have knocked them over. She began to tidy them up but stopped when she saw a pack that said, 'semi-permanent hair dye'.

She looked at herself in the mirror. Her long, blonde hair was a mess. It was straggly and matted. She sighed and examined the pack once more. She traced the label with her fingers and read the instructions. "Mmm..." The Murdochs wouldn't be looking for a young girl with short brown hair. She took a strand of her hair and placed it against the label. She read the words out loud in an American accent. "Hollywood Highlights – Deep Chestnut."

Spying a pair of scissors, she cut off long chunks of her hair. The blonde strands fell into the sink and soon spilled over onto the floor. She bundled the mess into a bin and rinsed her hair in the sink. She rubbed the dark brown paste into her scalp and looked at herself. Peat-coloured streams traced her cheeks and ran down her neck. She found a towel and rubbed them off. In a white cardboard box, the size of a packet of matches, she found a plastic bathing cap and pinged the elastic over her head. Now, she had to wait for ten minutes and then rinse again.

While she waited she plumped herself down on the big soft bed and looked out of one of the portholes. They were passing a massive green buoy with a walk-rail and lights. She could see another harbour full of dead boats, their carcasses all at different stages of decay. The spars of the boats jutted up from the water like the tattered ribcages of rotting whales. She thought of Harris and the ruined whaling stations. A shiver went down her spine and she turned away. As she stood up from the bed, however, she heard a splash. She looked down.

The river was flooding in over the carpet. At least an inch of dirty brown water covered her shoes.

"PAVEL!"

CHAPTER TWENTY-TWO
SOME OLD TROUBLE

Angus Murdoch lowered his binoculars and looked down the river. From where he was standing, on the old bridge nearest to the Clyde estuary, he could see that the cruiser had taken a knock before it had disappeared into a tangle of moored boats.

"What should we do, Dad?" asked Sandy. He wore a bandage over his wrist and his face had several large dollops of pink calamine lotion on it.

"*You* are going to do nothing. Can't be trusted."

"But, Dad..." began Sandy.

"You managed to burn down a million pound mart and let a couple of stupid kids escape."

"But..."

"And McGovern's going to be out of action for at least a month. So don't say another word."

Sandy Murdoch lowered his head to avoid the sneers of the local thugs who had gathered on the bridge.

"You lot." Angus Murdoch turned to the small gang of boys who'd gathered round them on the bridge. "Where are they now?"

The one called Flynn grabbed the binoculars.

He tried to focus. "Ah can't see them from here. But they must be well out into the Clyde."

"Are you sure it's them?" said Angus.

"Oh, it's them all right. Look guys, it's big lanky Pavel. He's come back to visit."

A murmur rose up from the group. Their white tracksuits fluttered in the morning breeze. "We've been up all night lookin' for those brats, Mr. Murdoch. If you want us to get them now, it'll cost you another hundred."

Angus Murdoch wished that McGovern had been there to keep these neds in check. "Fine. Go get them, Flynn. Hold them somewhere until tomorrow. I'll tell you what to do with them after that."

"An' a further hundred to work in daylight," said Flynn. "The police could nab us."

"Why, you..." Angus checked himself. "Fine!"

"Boys," said Flynn, "we'll need to borrow Big Burdie's boat."

The rest of the gang looked around nervously.

"If we damage that boat..." began one of the boys.

"Who's Burdie?" asked Sandy.

Flynn screwed up his eyes and sneered at Sandy. "You don't want to know. Okay?"

"You're dead right, we don't," said Angus, "Just stick to the plan, Flynn, and you'll get another hundred as a bonus."

"So that's three hundred extra, then?" pressed Flynn.

"As long as you keep them out of harm's way until twelve-noon, tomorrow."

"Aye, all right," he sighed. "If you insist."

"I insist," said Angus.

Sandy mooched along the bridge to his dad's waiting jeep.

"Dad, I could go with..."

"That lot?" Angus finished. "I don't think so."

As the Murdochs got into their jeep, the neds, led by Flynn, were already starting up a speedboat that had been moored under the bridge.

"We're going to the hospital to see Mr MacLeod," said Angus.

"Have you heard what's happened to mum? I still can't get her on the mobile," said Sandy.

"She flew into Glasgow last night with Pavel's father, by all accounts," snapped Angus.

"Pavel's father? What for?" asked Sandy.

"Your mother must have found the letters that I asked you to take with you. I wanted to keep her out of all this, and now, thanks to you..." Angus landed Sandy a cuff round the ear.

"Och!" Sandy ducked, nervously. "Da...ad," he complained.

"Get your seatbelt on and shut up."

"Only if you promise not to hit me any more." Sandy twitched as his dad showed him the palm of his hand.

Angus Murdoch pointed to the seatbelt. "Don't push your luck, son."

* * *

Jenny ran out onto the deck and found the cabin door. "Pavel, we're sinking!"

Pavel spun round and shrieked. "Aahh!"

Jenny froze; puzzled for a second before she remembered she had a bathing cap on and next to no hair. "Never mind this," she pinged the plastic cap off and pointed behind her, "there's water coming in downstairs."

Still staring in amazement at Jenny, Pavel edged past her and moved along the deck. As he did, the cruiser juddered. The stern lowered a few inches.

Lord barked and then tilted his head up at Jenny.

"Don't be scared," said Jenny, patting the old dog's soft coat.

"That knock must have been worse than I thought," said Pavel. He looked down the steps. Jenny moved in beside him. The water was gushing along the floor below. Pavel began searching the deck.

"What are you looking for?" asked Jenny.

"A lifebelt or a ring, or something..." Pavel broke off and dashed back into the cabin. The boat tilted further.

"I can't swim, Pavel!" screamed Jenny.

Pavel reappeared with a couple of bright orange lifejackets. His expression of relief, however, soon changed to one of horror. "It can't be..."

Jenny followed his gaze.

A yellow speedboat was racing towards them. "The police?" asked Jenny.

"Much worse," said Pavel. "Quick, get round the other side of the boat."

"Who is it, Pavel? They can help us," said Jenny.

"That's Big Burdie's boat," said Pavel.

Jenny could hear the fear in Pavel's voice. "Who's 'Big Burdie'? He sounds like a pantomime character." She slipped her lifejacket on and fastened the straps. Lord scampered round her legs.

"He got his name because he was never out of jail. You've heard of a jailbird before, haven't you?"

Jenny looked blankly at Pavel, still not sure what he meant.

"Obviously not. Okay, he's huge and he's the local gangster down here."

"Why would he be after us?" said Jenny.

Pavel scrunched up his eyes and stared into the morning sun. The speedboat, silhouetted by the dazzling sheen from the water, swung round them and came into full view.

It drew in closer.

"PAVEL!" cried a voice.

Jenny ducked down with Pavel. "They know your name?" she whispered.

Pavel's face was pure white. "It's Flynn. It's Gerry Flynn."

The cruiser lurched and the bow swung out of the water.

Jenny and Pavel were pitched into the Clyde.

Jenny felt the cold hit her as she plunged beneath the waves. Bubbles flew past her face as the life jacket pulled her back to the surface. She gasped for breath.

Hands caught hold of her jacket and lifted her from the river.

"You know, we should just leave you in the Clyde, Pavel. The water would have killed you in a few hours anyway. Save us doin' the job." Flynn's laugh was high-pitched and manic. His cronies joined in.

A big, skinny boy threw Pavel down at Flynn's feet.

"How's the arm, Pavel?" said Flynn.

Jenny remembered Pavel showing her the damage Flynn had inflicted on him previously.

Pavel ignored Flynn and shuffled in beside Jenny.

"Where's Lord?" screamed Jenny. She couldn't stop shivering.

"There's a dug in the drink," said one of the smaller neds.

"Just leave it," said Flynn. "If it swims hard enough, it

might make the animal home at Milton." The rest of the gang bellowed and taunted Lord as he swam round the speedboat.

"Help him into the boat!" yelled Jenny.

"Take us in towards the harbour," said Flynn, "we'll hold them there at the old terminal."

"Let the dog come on the boat," said Pavel.

His plea, however, was answered with a sharp kick in the ribs from Flynn.

"LORD!" shouted Jenny.

The speedboat's bow lifted as the powerful engine churned the water behind them.

Pavel caught Jenny's arm. "We're only a few hundred yards from the shore. He can still make it."

"He's too old," whispered Jenny. "He's too old to make it." She stared at the lone outline of Lord in the dark water, his front paws thrashing against the upturned hull of their cruiser. On the hills behind, a huge bank of giant windmills spun slowly in the morning breeze.

CHAPTER TWENTY-THREE
THE TUNNEL

Angus Murdoch stepped out of the jeep and looked back at his son. The hospital car park was full so he'd double-parked beside a large tree on a criss-cross of yellow lines. "Stay in the jeep and don't move," he grunted.

Sandy unclipped his seatbelt and shimmied across the leather upholstery. "Dad, what are you going to do?"

"I will do whatever I have to do to secure our future. The wind farm has to go ahead."

"Is Hamish MacLeod in there? Are you going to try and talk to him?" asked Sandy.

Angus shook his head dolefully. "That's right, Sandy. I'm going to have a chat with Mr MacLeod."

Sandy squinted up at the black brick buildings.

"How are you going to find him? Are you sure you don't want me to come with you?"

"Just stay put. Keep an eye out for Jenny and Pavel," snapped Angus.

"But, Flynn will have..."

"Just do it!" shouted Angus.

Angus looked back at the hospital buildings.

He had to do this alone. He had to see if there was any way he could stop Hamish MacLeod from ruining his plans. Glancing back one more time to check that Sandy was still in the jeep, Angus wandered through a cluster of patients, staff and visitors, all puffing on their cigarettes at the main entrance. He looked up at a board that read 'Cardiology' and checked that the gloves were still in his inside pocket. He took a deep breath then continued down the polished corridor.

* * *

It was pitch dark in the tunnel but Jenny could hear Pavel shuffling about ten yards away. "What are you doing, Pavel?" she asked. Her teeth were chattering.

"I want to hear what they're saying," he whispered.

She shuffled along beside him. Outside the tunnel Jenny could hear Flynn arguing with one of the other neds.

Pavel let out a sigh. "Typical."

"What's typical?" said Jenny.

"Flynn's decided that one of his creeps has a better jacket than him, and he wants it."

There was a loud bang at the end of the tunnel, followed by a barrage of shouts and swearing. Jenny heard Flynn laugh and say, "That's better. It's mine now, so take your eyes off."

The shouts and curses eventually died down until there was no sound except for an occasional drip of water.

"I want to see if there's any way out of here before they come back, before we freeze to death. They're probably off taking Big Burdie's boat back to its mooring. We don't have much time."

Jenny heard something. "Quiet, Pavel."

A far-off bark echoed down the tunnel.

"LORD!" shouted Jenny.

Pavel called out too. "Lord! Lord! We're in here, boy."

The barking grew more intense. *It's definitely him*, decided Jenny. There was always a raspy growl before every yelp, like someone revving up an engine before it backfired.

There was a loud bashing sound at the far end of the tunnel again.

"There must be a metal door down there. Come on, Jenny, take my hand."

Jenny felt Pavel's hand press into hers.

Ahead, there was another clatter of something smashing into metal.

A thin crack of light split the darkness.

Jenny winced.

"Watch where you're putting your feet," said Pavel. "There's lots of rubbish in here."

Jenny caught her shin on something cold and hard. She reached down and traced her fingers along the length of a wooden shaft until she felt the handle. "It's a spade," she whispered.

"Take it with us," said Pavel.

Woof!

Jenny moved forward, waving the shovel before her like a mine detector. "Lord!"

Pavel reached the crack of light first. Jenny could see Lord's outline flickering across the bright white line ahead. She banged her shoulder off the metal and pushed her fingers through the narrow gap. She felt Lord's tongue wetting her fingertips.

"Thank God," she moaned, already weeping with relief.

"Hand me the shovel," said Pavel.

Jenny gave him the shovel and stood back a little as Pavel wedged it into the gap. They both leaned on the handle and pushed hard. The slash of light widened until they could see a tall stone monument.

"What's that?" asked Jenny.

"I don't know," said Pavel, "but I remember seeing it from the train. We're still near the river and the railway track. I think I know where we are."

"Push harder!" said Jenny. She put her whole weight on the handle of the spade, wedging the gap open even further.

Crack!

The gap closed over.

"No!" she wailed. "The spade's broken."

"Nice one, Jenny. That was the final straw."

"Don't..." Jenny clenched her fists. "Don't start with the stupid sayings, okay?"

"Got it," moaned Pavel.

"Pavel..."

"No, I understand," he chuckled. "Least said, soonest mended."

She landed him a punch.

Pavel's stupid giggle filled the dark tunnel.

"How can you laugh at a time like this?" asked Jenny. "My father's in hospital and we've no way of getting the letter to him in time unless we get out of here."

Lord's paws scratched the outer surface of the metal plate that blocked their way out. A woeful whine filled their ears.

"You've still got the letter then?" said Pavel. Jenny searched her belt and sighed as she felt the smooth surface of the envelope. Suddenly a thought occurred to her and she stuck her hand in the pocket of her jeans. "I have Windy's mobile number."

"So," said Pavel, in a derisory tone.

"So, maybe we can call him," she snapped.

"Oh yeah... There's a whole bank of phones down here and Flynn's dropped his mobile..."

"What is it?" said Jenny.

"Flynn. He was scuffling around with that other ned." Pavel pushed his eye against the crack of light. "You're a genius, Jenny."

"I am?" she asked.

"Yes, you are. Flynn's dumped his jacket on the ground. I can see it. Far too pleased with his new one, he's gone off without it. I wonder..."

Jenny pressed her eye against the crack of light.

She could just make out an off-white shell suit top lying scrunched up on the ground about two yards away from the metal plate.

Pavel took the broken handle of the spade and forced it through the crack until it opened up another few inches.

"Can you reach it, Jenny?"

"I'm not sticking my arm through there. If that old handle breaks the metal plate will cut my arm off."

"And...?" said Pavel, straining with the handle.

"And, I suppose I could try." Jenny rolled up her sleeve and eased her hand through the gap. "It's too far away. Flynn isn't daft. He won't have left his mobile in there."

"He's not that clever either," said Pavel. "He didn't know that Lord would come back, did he? Can you get Lord to bring it closer?"

Jenny had no idea if Lord had the brains to do this. "Lord," she shouted. "Bring the jacket!"

Lord wagged his tail and shook more river water from his coat.

"Lord, where's the sweetie? Where's the chocolate?"

Lord yelped and sniffed the ground around his front paws.

"There it is!" said Jenny, in a high-pitched, anxious voice.

Lord's tail windmilled even faster. The dog sniffed Flynn's white top.

"That's it, boy. That's where the sweetie is!" Lord put the shell suit top in his mouth and shook it. It flew free of his jaws and landed much closer to the gap in the metal plate.

Jenny pushed her arm out as far as she could. Her fingers brushed against the slippery material. Cold and slightly damp, Flynn's jacket seemed to jump away from her.

Lord caught hold of it and shook it again.

"No!" yelled Jenny. "Bring it here!"

Lord turned his back on her and dug into the soil underneath the jacket. A white lump of cloth whisked up into the air amongst a spray of dirt, and battered against the gap. Something hard hit the metal plate. Jenny pushed her eye against the gap and spied the black mobile on the ground.

"Quickly," said Pavel, "I'm struggling to keep it open." The wooden handle creaked like an old door and the gap wavered.

Jenny jabbed her arm through the gap as near to the ground as she could.

"Hey!" a voice rose up from the distance. "There's a dug up at the tunnel!"

Jenny fumbled for the phone.

Pavel slipped. "Jenny, I can't hold it any..."

Jenny began to pull her arm back.

The wooden handle snapped with a loud crack and the gap sprang shut.

"ARGH!"

"Jenny!" yelled Pavel.

Jenny whimpered quietly.

Pavel put his arm around her. "Jenny?"

"I've got it," said Jenny. She handed Pavel the phone.

"Thank God," said Pavel. "Flynn's realised he's left it behind. We've only got a minute before they get back here." In the dim light, he glanced down at Jenny's arm. "Are you okay? I thought you had..."

"I'm fine, but Lord is out there with those idiots."

"Let's phone Windy," said Pavel.

They edged back from the narrow gap and held up the slip of paper with Windy's number on it. There was just enough light to read it so Pavel switched on the mobile and dialled. Jenny waited.

"There's no answer," said Pavel.

"Leave a message," urged Jenny.

"Hold on," said Pavel. "This is Flynn's phone, right?"

Jenny nodded. "That was definitely his jacket."

"I've got an idea," said Pavel, a wry smile forming on his face. He typed into the phone.

CHAPTER TWENTY-FOUR
EVIL INTENT

They had just enough time to put the mobile back in Flynn's pocket and flick the jacket away from the gap in the metal door.

"Quick," whispered Pavel. "We need to get back down the tunnel to where Flynn left us or he'll be suspicious."

They both plumped down just as the big heavy door swung inwards.

"Torture time!" cried Flynn, in a happy-go-lucky kind of voice.

"That Murdoch bloke said we shouldn't hurt them. Said we just had to keep them here for a bit and then..."

"Shut it, Colie!" barked Flynn.

The one called Colie shrugged his shoulders and pulled his hoodie further down over his eyes.

Lord whined and then produced his customary growl-come-woof.

"You'd better let us go," said Jenny, still wincing in the bright light.

"Ha! Listen to her," said Flynn.

The rest of the group laughed on cue.

"Look at them: Pavel the Pole and his little Highland girlfriend."

Pavel stiffened. "Leave her alone, Flynn."

"What's wrong, Pav, can ye no think of a witty sayin' to make us laugh? Let me see..." Flynn scrunched up Pavel's face with a big meaty hand and grinned. "How about, 'better the devil you know'?" Pavel pulled his head away from Flynn's grip.

Jenny saw Lord outside, being held by several of the yobs. One of them bolted forward and handed Flynn his old jacket. Flynn retrieved his mobile and threw the jacket back at the ned.

"Bring them up to the tower," said Flynn.

What Flynn called the tower was actually the big stone monument they'd seen earlier. It reminded Jenny of the Needlestone that sat above Hushwish Bay. She wished she was still there, huddled in out of the wind with her father and Lord, looking down on their sheep.

"Hurry it up, boys," said Flynn. "Tie them to the tower and we'll see if they can take the usual treatment."

Jenny didn't like the sound of this at all and she could see that Pavel was visibly shaking at the prospect.

They were dragged up a small hill behind what looked like an abandoned castle until they arrived at the base of the red sandstone monument.

Flynn ordered his thugs to tie them to it. "You see, Pav, you managed to get me expelled from school. And I've never been the same since. It was you who set me on this path of gratuitous violence and adventure." Flynn spoke with the annoying twang of a pirate. "You see, there's a lot to thank you for, Pav. I almost made the trip up to wherever it is you hide these days to sort you out myself, but there's so much to do down here these days and..." Flynn stopped mid-flow. He screwed up his eyes. "Why does Murdoch want you two out o' the way so much? He never told us the real reason."

Pavel shrugged.

Flynn beamed and addressed his gang. "Did you see that, boys? He doesn't want to tell me."

Jenny scanned the horizon for any sign of Windy or the police.

"Bring out the hose," said Flynn.

The boy called Colie trailed out a long length of black, rubber hose.

Flynn picked up the end and sniffed it. He screwed up his face and faked a retch. "Do you see that big circle of gravel down there, Pav?"

Jenny and Pavel looked over Flynn's shoulders.

"That's the sewage plant," said Flynn. "And this... this is the waste hose."

The gang rattled with laughter.

"We once covered a captive in the stuff, head to foot, and then left him for the seagulls tae pick at for three days."

Jenny strained on the rope.

Lord barked, as if knowing what Flynn was threatening.

"So, let me ask you one more time, Pav... why is Murdoch chasing you? Why has he asked us to keep you here? What's the money at stake, because there's always money behind this kind of thing?"

"It's all about those things behind you," said Jenny, desperately trying to stall for time.

Flynn turned. "What things?"

"The windmills," said Pavel.

"The windmills?" repeated Flynn, in a nasally, childlike

tone. "You'll have to do better than that." He signalled one of his cronies to couple the hose to an outlet on the concrete wall several feet below the monument. A more substantial pipe led all the way back to the sewage pit. "No," said Jenny, "it's the truth. They're going to build windmills on our land and we're trying to stop them."

Flynn leaned into Jenny's face. "Why?"

She could smell his bad breath.

"Because our land is beautiful," said Jenny. Her voice was thin and full of fear.

"Because they ruin the environment," said Pavel. "They kill birds and..."

"Kill birds?" screeched Flynn. "We kill birds. Who cares about a few birds?" Flynn paused to stare at the long row of giant windmills on the horizon. "You know, you've given me an idea."

Pavel found Jenny's hand behind his back and squeezed it reassuringly.

Flynn turned back to face them and continued, "I think we should take you across the Clyde and climb up to one of those things. I never really appreciated them before. They're a bloomin' work of art, Pav. But I reckon I could improve them a bit."

"How's that then, big man," said the snivelling Colie.

Flynn lashed out at his minion and then turned back to face Jenny. "We could tie these two onto the sails and watch them spin, and spin, and spin..."

"Aye!" clamoured the gang.

"You're a genius," said Colie.

Flynn slapped Colie across the head. "Shut it, Colie."

Colie ducked and then cringed like a naughty puppy.

"Here's what we'll do," said Flynn. "We'll cover them in the gunk, drag them across the water and then tie them to the sails of that big windmill over there. Let them spin dry."

"Now you're talkin', Big Ma..."

Flynn scowled at Colie. "Stop calling me, 'Big Man', or we'll test it out on you first."

Jenny could see why Flynn might be annoyed at the name. He was only a little taller than her; muscle-bound, but short.

"Okay," shouted Flynn, "turn on the gunk! Let 'em have it!"

An excited-looking yob in black pushed down on a long rusty handle next to the coupling.

"Wait!" shouted a voice.

The boy hesitated.

Flynn spun round.

Pavel gripped Jenny's hand even tighter.

Jenny had hoped it was Windy, coming to the rescue, but it wasn't. This man was much bigger. "Who's that?" she whispered.

"It's Big Burdie," Pavel whispered back. "Flynn's had it now."

* * *

In the hospital, Angus Murdoch walked down the bright corridor. Sunshine poured in through the full-length windows on either side of him, and his collar was wet with sweat. As he walked, he pulled on a pair of blue plastic gloves and then surreptitiously stuck his hands back into the pockets of his heavy jacket. His mind was racing. *I should never have brought my jeep to the hospital car park. I should never have left Sandy to look out for Jenny MacLeod and Pavel. Where is Ellen? Will I turn a corner and bump into her, have to explain the whole thing? I'm going to have to do it.*

"Can I help you, sir?" said a nurse dressed in navy and white. She fumbled for a watch in her pocket.

Angus stumbled awkwardly over his words,

"I... I'm fine." He could feel his face flush hot.

"You look a little anxious. Are you sure you're okay?" she pressed.

"I'm fine, I said." He pushed past her and scanned the signs ahead before staring back at her. The nurse was standing stalk-still in the middle of the corridor, holding her watch, cocking her head suspiciously at him. He turned the corner into the ward and waited a moment. *Is she following me?*

He pictured Hamish MacLeod's face. It flickered in his head like an old movie reel, his neighbour's different expressions eventually all merging into one of complete and utter loathing. Angus's temples were burning, his chest so tight that every breath was a judder. He was mumbling to himself, "If I have to do it, I will. I've come this far and nothing is going to get in my way now."

He saw the sign that read, 'Coronary Care'. MacLeod was supposed to be in the last bed on the ward. There were six beds to his left and four beds to his right. What had they meant? Was it the left or the right? He tried to pick Hamish out. He didn't recognise anyone. Then he saw it. The last bed on the right had a curtain pulled round it. That had to be it. With any luck he'd be out cold.

The wind farm would go ahead. He would be rid of any interference. They would just think Hamish had died naturally. All he had to do was pinch the plastic tube that fed him the oxygen. All the men in here had a similar tube. He knew which one it was.

Angus took a deep breath and then flicked open the curtain.

CHAPTER TWENTY-FIVE
FRAMED

The man known as Big Burdie climbed the hill, followed by a mean-looking retinue of his own. He clutched a mobile phone in his right hand, holding it before him like a holy object.

"Flynn!" he bellowed. "What have you done to ma speedboat?"

Jenny saw Flynn's gang melt away into the undergrowth.

"S...s...speedboat?" stuttered Flynn.

"The one you stole from me and then scratched," bellowed Big Burdie, closing in fast.

Flynn looked round in desperation for his gang. "The boys are puttin' it back right now," said Flynn.

Jenny could tell by the bully's voice that he was terrified.

"So, let me get this straight, Flynn, you found my speedboat, did ye? Just lying around, up for grabs?" Big Burdie looked like a wrestler: bald, built like a tank and plastered in tattoos. He walked with the wide, lumbering gate of a gorilla.

Flynn backed off as Burdie reached the monument. The big man's henchmen spread out behind him.

"Who are these runts?" said Burdie, pointing at Jenny and Pavel.

"We're keeping them s...s...safe," stammered Flynn, obviously under pressure.

Lord appeared at the edge of the bushes. He raised his hackles and began barking.

Big Burdie pulled a gun from his jacket and pointed it at Lord.

"Stop!" yelled Jenny.

Without taking his eyes off Lord, Big Burdie talked out of the side of his mouth, "Tell it to stay, hen."

Jenny snapped her head around until she faced Lord and shouted, "STAY!"

Lord stopped barking and, to Jenny's amazement, sat down.

"Well done," said big Burdie. He lowered his aim.

"You're speedboat's going to take a bit of fixing," said Pavel.

Flynn froze on the spot, then yelled, "What? Liar!"

Big Burdie lifted his aim and Flynn backed away a few more steps.

"He's lying!" Flynn complained.

"Flynn rammed us. Hit us square on and sank us," said Pavel.

"Look," gasped Jenny, "you can still see a bit of our boat." She nodded out into the Clyde.

Big Burdie followed Jenny's stare and caught Flynn by the throat. He shoved the screen of his Blackberry in front of Flynn's face. "This is your text but I don't think it was meant for me."

Flynn tried to speak but he couldn't.

"You thought you were texting Sandy," Big Burdie tilted his head like a raptor about to bite, "whoever Sandy is..."

Jenny bit her lip in an effort not to smile.

Big Burdie screwed up his face and read out the rest of the message, "We nicked Big Turdie's vomit-yellow speedboat and rammed the cruiser in the Clyde, so job done. I'll get gang to take the speedboat back before the big numpty sees the damage."

Flynn tried to free himself. "That wasn't me. I've been framed!"

Big Burdie closed his massive fingers round Flynn's throat and then tossed him towards one of his henchmen. "Take him back to base until I see the speedboat for myself. In fact..." Big Burdie seemed to change his mind, "if there's a single scratch on the paintwork..." Big Burdie drew his forefinger over his throat in a horrible slashing motion and then flicked the struggling Flynn away.

"It's a set-up!" screamed Flynn. "I'll get you back, Pavel!" His eyes were full of fear.

Jenny saw Pavel wiggle his fingers into a wave. He winked at Flynn at the same time.

Flynn erupted, but was instantly smacked quiet by one of Big Burdie's henchmen.

Jenny shrank back from the big man who now circled them.

"I had Flynn down as a thief and a bully, not a pirate." The big man began to untie them.

"He just rammed us," said Jenny.

"We took on water and had to swim for it," said Pavel.

Big Burdie eyed them suspiciously. "So, what were you two doing on a cruiser?"

"Trying to get away from him," said Pavel, pointing to where Big Burdie's men were bundling Flynn into the back seat of a silver Hummer.

"I don't know what Flynn is up to," said Big Burdie, throwing their ropes away from the base of the monument, "but he's acting without my permission. So, as far as I'm concerned, you two..." Big Burdie squinted at Lord, "...and your old dug can go."

"You won't really hurt him, will you?" asked Jenny, staring down at Flynn.

Pavel widened his eyes at her in warning.

Big Burdie looked at Jenny carefully. "He's blood. My sister's boy." Big Burdie looked out at the hull of the upturned cruiser. "Unfortunately," he added.

"Jean! Tom!"

Jenny's heart lifted. It was Windy.

Big Burdie had already begun to walk down the hill.

Jenny saw that Windy was about to challenge the big man. "No Windy! We're okay!" She frantically waved Windy away from Big Burdie.

Pavel joined in, moving his hands, palms outstretched, in a 'please, whatever you do, don't do that' kind of way.

Windy seemed to understand, choosing to sidestep Big Burdie rather than confront him.

Big Burdie marched past.

Lord barked and raced towards Windy. Windy smiled and then did a double take. He pointed at Jenny. "Your hair..."

"Oh," said Jenny, having completely forgotten about cutting her hair and then dying it dark brown, "I just fancied a change."

"It suits you," said Windy, looking completely bemused. "Well, I was on the hills above Loch Lomond, looking at a new wind farm site, when the signal on my mobile suddenly came back on. I got your text message. You said you were in trouble and... where's your father?"

Jenny hugged Windy. "Thanks for coming, Windy."

Pavel looked up at Dumbarton Rock and the valley beyond. "You're going to build more of those things on the hills around Loch Lomond?"

"They're looking at having hundreds and..."

"And you're quite happy with that are you?"

Windy shrugged. "Well, actually, I don't think it's the right place for them and..."

"Pavel!" snapped Jenny, "Say thanks to Windy for coming here straight away."

Windy looked puzzled. "Pavel?" He looked at Jenny. "Why are you calling him Pavel?"

Jenny caught her breath and then issued a long sigh. "And that's Lord," she said, "and I'm actually called Jenny MacLeod."

"Nice one, Jenny," murmured Pavel.

"I don't understand," said Windy. He took a step back from them. His smile had fallen. "Why did you...? And your father?"

"My father is in big trouble," said Jenny. She looked mournfully at Pavel.

The wind cut through the grass at their feet and the big windmills turned on the hills above the Clyde.

"I'm sorry," said Jenny.

"I'm just wondering what else I should know," said Windy.

Jenny looked at Pavel and nodded. "We need to tell Windy the whole lot. He's the only person who's helped us on this whole mad trip."

Windy looked expectantly at Pavel.

"Fine," Pavel blurted.

Jenny knelt down to pat Lord. "Look, Windy, can we tell you everything on our way to the hospital?"

"What's wrong with you?" he asked.

"We're fine," said Jenny. "As I said, it's my dad." She prized the scrunched-up envelope from behind her belt. "I need you to read this."

"And we need to explain why we don't want your wind farm in our bay," added Pavel.

Jenny glowered at Pavel.

Windy took the envelope and scratched his head. "Now, I'm very confused." He followed Jenny and Pavel down the path away from the monument. "What's this got to do with wind farms?"

"Everything," said Pavel, without looking back. "Absolutely everything."

"Jenny?" asked Windy.

"Yes, Windy?" answered Jenny.

Windy put his fingers inside the envelope. "Is there supposed to be something inside this envelope?"

Jenny grabbed the envelope back.

Pavel turned round, eyes wide. "Where is the letter?"

Jenny's mouth had fallen open. "It's gone, Pavel. The letter's gone." She began to sob.

CHAPTER TWENTY-SIX
THE RIGHT BED

Windy pulled into the massively overcrowded car park of the Royal Alexandra Hospital and dropped to first gear. Jenny could tell that the tall, straggly man, who'd been so kind to them for so much of their trip, was flagging. Their long-winded explanation about the protestors, her father's heart attack, and the Murdochs' deceit had shocked him.

"So you thought I would tell the police or something?" said Windy.

Pavel stared at Windy in the rear view mirror as they turned into a small road beneath a grassy slope. "So you would have helped us right from the start, then?" asked Pavel. "No questions asked?"

"Well," considered Windy, "I didn't really know you at all back at Tarbert, did I? I might have considered it and..."

"No, I thought not," interrupted Pavel.

Windy pulled on the handbrake and squinted up the hill at the high hospital buildings.

Jenny felt her heart race at the prospect of seeing her father. She didn't even know if he was still alive.

Pavel grabbed her shoulder as she made to open the car

door. "The Murdochs are bound to be watching this place. We should split up."

"But my hair," said Jenny. "They'll never recognise me like this."

"It's not enough," said Pavel. "We'll stick out like a sore thumb."

Windy caught hold of Lord's lead. "Look Jenny, there's a wheel chair across there. Put Pavel in it and push him into the hospital. I'll stay here with Lord, make sure no-one is following you."

"You do know how stupid that sounds, don't you?" said Pavel.

"Pavel," snapped Jenny, "Windy's only trying to help."

Pavel sighed. "No wonder, it's like some kind of 'Carry On' film or something. You can't just nick a wheel chair and..."

"Well, I think it's a good idea," said Jenny, "so are you coming or not, because I'm going to find my dad?"

"Fine!" Pavel shrugged.

Windy gave them the thumbs-up as they wandered up the slope towards the wheelchair. "What's a wheelchair doing round the back of the hospital anyway?" asked Pavel. "I mean, just abandoned like that?"

"I don't know," said Jenny. She saw Windy get out of the car and take Lord round the edge of the car park.

Pavel caught hold of the wheel chair and rolled it along the tarmac. "It's broken. Look, the wheel's buckled."

"It's not too bad," said Jenny. She pointed to a glass door. "Let's wheel it in there. That could be Dad's ward."

"I doubt it," said Pavel, "it says 'Maternity' on that sign up there." There was a blue sign with a series of arrows underneath listing wards 2-8.

"Get in, then," said Jenny.

Reluctantly, Pavel edged into the black, canvas seat and hunkered down. He grabbed a blanket from a washing trolley and threw it over his knees.

They made their way through a series of corridors until they saw another building across a walkway.

A nurse passed by.

"Excuse me," said Jenny, "can you tell us where the heart patients are?"

The nurse seemed to be in a rush. She flicked her fingers at the building opposite. "In there."

They were just about to cross an open walkway when Pavel grabbed the rim of the wheels and brought the chair to a skidding stop. "Wait!"

Jenny saw a jeep parked on the criss-cross yellow lines. "That's the Murdoch's jeep."

"And Sandy's sitting in it," said Pavel. "He's watching the walkway."

"We have to go across," said Jenny. "I think Angus Murdoch will do anything to stop Dad interfering with his plans."

"Brilliant!" said Pavel.

"What is it?" Jenny whispered. "He's seen us."

Sandy Murdoch had slid out of the jeep. He was peering in their direction.

"Ignore him," said Pavel, "and push me across the walkway."

Jenny turned her face away from Sandy and walked resolutely across the walkway. The buckled wheel caused the chair to lift and fall with every step. "He's seen someone else. He's gone back into the jeep," said Pavel. "He took a look all right, but I think your hair fooled him."

Several doctors in white coats swished past them, walking in the opposite direction.

"I don't like it, Jenny. Where's Angus Murdoch?" said Pavel.

"Where's my dad?" said Jenny. "What are we going to do without the letter?"

Ahead, they saw a sign that read 'Coronary Care'.

"That's it," said Pavel. "He has to be in there."

"Left or right?" said Jenny.

Pavel stood up out of the chair. "There are fewer beds on the right. Let's try the one with the curtain round it."

Jenny could see that someone was behind the curtain. She saw their big feet. The green, plastic curtain bulged from within, as if someone was trying to get out.

"Dad?" she whispered, sharply.

Something heavy clattered to the floor and a man cursed.

"Dad!" she shouted.

Pavel ran forward with her and swished open the curtain. "Hey!"

A large man in a white coat was struggling with a gas canister.

Pavel and Jenny stared down at the empty bed.

The man backed off, clutching his chest. "You gave me the fright of my life."

"Where's he gone?" Jenny pointed to the bed. The linen was crumpled and she could still see the impression of a body on the fitted sheet.

"Never made it..." The man hesitated. "I'm sorry. Did you know him?"

"Who was it?" asked Pavel.

The man read the sign above the bed: "Mr H Johnston."

Jenny began to cry.

"I'm sorry," said the man, "I shouldn't have blurted it out like that. You know, the bit about him passing away and stuff. I'm just changing the oxygen canisters."

"We didn't know him," whimpered Jenny. "It's just that we've been on such a terrible journey and..."

"We're looking for Mr MacLeod," said Pavel.

"Now, you're the second person who's mentioned him in the space of about two minutes," said the man.

"What did the other person look like?" asked Jenny.

"Oh, he was big, well-dressed. Had the same accent as you; kind of soft and lilting."

"Did you tell him where Mr. MacLeod was?" asked Pavel, his voice strong and accusatory.

"Well, yes... he's one floor above, in the pre-op ward. He's just about to have his operation."

Jenny and Pavel spun round and skidded off back down the corridor they'd just come up.

"That man," shouted the porter, "the one who asked about MacLeod... he looked terrible. All sweating and stuff," he continued. "I told him he should get one of the doctors to have a look at him. But by then he was talking to himself, and..."

The man's words tailed off as Jenny and Pavel broke into a run and made for the stairs. Jumping them two at a time, they reached the upper landing and burst through the swing doors, colliding with a nurse carrying a box of pills, causing them to scatter all over the floor like tiny marbles. "Stop running!" she yelled.

Jenny ignored her and pelted round the corner, checking every bed as she passed. They saw the sign that read 'Pre-Op' at the end of the first row of beds. Jenny ducked under the grasping arms of a portly cleaning lady dressed in purple and stepped under the sign.

"Hey there. Slow down!" she yelled.

Jenny steadied herself on the wall before looking up.

Behind her, Pavel shouted, "It's him!"

Jenny rubbed her eyes.

Pavel dodged the cleaning lady and caught hold of Jenny's arm. "It's Murdoch!"

CHAPTER TWENTY-SEVEN
THE SHOWDOWN

Jenny saw the unmistakable figure of Angus Murdoch stooping over the bed at the end of the corridor. Sporting a pair of blue, plastic gloves, Murdoch was pinching down hard on the clear plastic tube that hung down from the wall.

The man in the bed was kicking against his sheets.

Jenny couldn't speak. Her mouth was completely dry. Her heart pounded hard against her chest.

Pavel shouted out, "Stop it!"

Murdoch ducked down in fright, pulling the plastic tube right out of the wall.

The man in the bed gasped for air.

"ENOUGH!" bellowed a voice.

Angus Murdoch stood up and backed off. He looked terrified.

Jenny couldn't see who'd shouted out; she could only think about getting to the bed.

Three people stepped in through a fire exit as Jenny and Pavel stumbled to a halt.

Nurses and doctors were running down the corridor behind them, but Jenny couldn't take her eyes off the man in the bed.

"Dad?" she shouted.

Weakly, the man in the bed raised his hand.

"Dad!" shouted Pavel.

Jenny was confused.

Pavel's dad stepped forward and caught hold of Angus Murdoch's collar. He yanked him down to the floor. Jenny saw Angus look up in surprise, but, as he did, Mrs Murdoch stepped forward and slapped her husband full on the face.

Jenny and Pavel tried to wriggle free of the hands that held them from behind. "It's my dad in that bed," said Jenny. "He can't breathe. Let me go!"

As the various fingers loosened their grip on her clothes, Jenny sprinted forward. Without waiting, she picked up the plastic tube and shoved it over a nozzle on the wall that was hissing gas. She spun round and stared down her dad's face. She heard him take a deep breath before his big hands pulled her closer.

"Jenny..."

"Dad, it's okay," she sobbed. Her hands found the edge of his gown. Through her tears she squinted up at the third figure, the other person who was standing next to Mrs Murdoch and Pavel's dad. She recognised the woman but she couldn't remember from where. Jenny loosened her grip on her dad's gown as the doctors moved in beside her. "Dad? I want to be with my dad!"

"He'll be all right, love," said a nurse.

Hamish MacLeod took another deep breath and then let out a long sigh. His head plopped back onto his pillow.

Jenny made to rush forward again but the mystery woman

caught hold of her arm and led her back from the bed.

Several men barged in past them and caught hold of Angus Murdoch. Pavel's dad let go his hold and watched as the mish-mash of porters and doctors pulled Murdoch away from the bed.

"I only did it for you, Ellen!" whimpered Murdoch.

"You did it for yourself, you greedy fool!" screamed Mrs Murdoch. "You would have killed Hamish if we hadn't got here in time." Tears rolled down Ellen Murdoch's face.

"Ellen..." pleaded Mr Murdoch.

"Get out of my sight," she hissed.

Mr Murdoch's wounded expression instantly changed into one of absolute rage. He stared like a madman up at the clock on the wall. "It's too late now, Hamish! It's after twelve noon. The bank won't give you your money now! The wind farm will go ahead whether you like it or not!"

"No it won't," said Mrs Murdoch.

Mr Murdoch's face assumed a puzzled expression as Mrs Murdoch pulled out a bundle of letters. "I've been to the bank on Hamish's behalf and they're holding his money in a high-interest account."

Jenny saw her dad's eyes blink open. "What money? I don't under..."

Now that Murdoch was out of the way, Jenny moved forward and pressed her wet cheek against her dad's open hand. "It's all right, Dad. Everything's going to be all right."

Jenny squinted up at Pavel. He was staring at the woman with the grey hair. Jenny narrowed her eyes. "I know you, don't I?"

The scrawny-looking woman nodded. "I'm sorry, if I hurt you the last time we met."

Jenny's heart sank like a lump of lead. "You're the protestor from the beach. You put your hand over my mouth. If it wasn't for you my dad wouldn't be in here!" Jenny stiffened and faced the woman.

The woman was shocked. "No... That's not..."

"Go on, get out of here! Haven't you done enough?" Jenny stood up and made to push her away, but Pavel stepped in front of her.

"Pavel, get out my way. This woman..."

Jenny watched in amazement as Pavel caught hold of the woman's hand. Jenny felt her face flush.

"This woman is my mum," Pavel finished.

"Your what?" said Jenny. Her head was thumping. Her mind was full of crashing waves, huge, white windmills and the angry faces of the protestors they'd encountered on Hushwish Bay. Jenny let go her dad's hand and walked towards Pavel. Even more tears filled her eyes as her overwhelming relief turned to anger.

"You tricked me."

"I didn't. I..."

"Yes you did. You used me to help your mad mum here get her way. You were only worried about the wind farm."

Pavel's mum looked shaken. "He didn't use you."

Jenny looked into the woman's light-grey eyes. "You've filled his head with all your rubbish. This was probably your plan all along."

The rotund figure of Mrs Murdoch stepped in beside Pavel's mum and dad. Her eyes were streaming with tears. "Jenny. The only person that had any kind of a plan was that stupid, greedy husband of mine. If it wasn't for Pavel, we wouldn't have known about the letters, about your mother's insurance money."

Now that Mr Murdoch was safely out of the ward, the porters returned and adjusted her dad's bed.

"Yes, but..." Jenny felt totally betrayed.

"Jenny?"

She recognised her father's voice. "Dad?" Jenny found his hand again and squeezed it.

"Go easy on them, Jenny," he whispered.

"But, Dad... it's all been..."

"You're here. That's all that matters," he whispered.

Pavel wiped his face with his sleeve. "Jenny?"

"Don't..." she gasped.

"Come on, Jenny. It's not what you think. I was only trying to help and..."

"Don't ever speak to me again, Pavel."

Jenny made way for two doctors who appeared at the bedside. They took her dad's pulse and nodded.

Pavel's father took a deep breath and looked into Jenny's eyes. He spoke in his soft Polish accent. "Pavel's a good boy. He looked after you, didn't he?"

A couple of porters clicked the wheels down on her dad's bed and wheeled him towards the operating theatre.

A doctor knelt and spoke to Jenny. "This is going to take four or five hours. Your dad should be fine, though. Try not to worry."

Jenny ran ahead and stopped the trolley. She bent over and kissed her dad's forehead. "I love you, Dad," she whispered.

"And I love you too, Jenny," he whispered back. "Thanks for coming to see me."

Jenny watched helplessly, as her dad's trolley rolled forward again.

"Hey!" yelled a sharp voice. "You can't come in here with that."

Jenny braced, half-expecting to see Angus Murdoch again.

Woof!

Jenny found a smile, as a bedraggled Windy skidded round the corner of the ward after Lord.

The old dog ran straight up to her dad and licked his fingers.

"Oh, so you made it all the way here too, did you? Good boy, good boy..." her dad whispered.

Jenny hugged Lord as the porters wheeled her dad into the bright lights of the operating theatre. He had a contented smile on his face.

The doors swung shut and Lord nuzzled in.

His wet nose was cold against her neck.

CHAPTER TWENTY-EIGHT
THE SUMMER WIND

The sun had punched a perfect hole in the powder-blue sky. Jenny felt its warmth on her face as she looked up at the Needlestone that stood above Hushwish Bay.

"I bet that big obelisk was an eyesore in its day," said Pavel.

Jenny ran forward and traced its rough surface with her fingertips and grinned. "I doubt it."

"No, Pavel's right, Jenny. I bet there was more than a wee bit of trouble from the locals when they erected this monstrosity." Her dad moved in beside her and craned up to look at its highest point.

Jenny looked down at Lord, whisking round her father's feet, snapping at his laces. They all turned to look out over the bay and Lord plumped down on her dad's left foot. "We kept it the way mum would have wanted it," said Jenny.

"We did, Jenny, we did. But I still think we were right to let them go ahead."

Pavel kicked a few loose stones down the hill and watched them roll. "They're not that bad, I suppose."

"See," said Jenny, triumphantly. "I told you Windy would find a better spot for them."

"And only the three, not six," said Hamish.

"Only the three," repeated Pavel.

Hamish flicked Lord off his foot and led them around the Needlestone. "You really feel like this place is your home now, don't you, Pavel?"

"The minute I came to Harris I knew I was home. Home is where the heart is." He laughed.

Jenny shook her head. "What's going to happen to the Murdochs, Dad?"

They began to climb the steep slope behind the Needle-stone.

Her dad sighed. "Mr Murdoch's in a lot of trouble. He owes a fortune to the Oban Mart."

"But you dropped all the charges against him, Mr MacLeod," said Pavel.

"Putting him in jail wouldn't have brought the mart back, and besides... Mrs Murdoch's a better jail-keeper than most."

"Sandy's been grounded for a year," chuckled Pavel.

"And Angus for about ten, I would say," said her dad.

A skein of geese flapped a noisy path over the headland and then banked east towards the Isle of Skye. The heather at their feet trembled in the breeze and Jenny pointed down at the crags. "It's the peregrine falcon again, Dad."

"So it is," said her father.

The falcon sliced through the air above the crags, then folded its wings in tight for a dive. It disappeared out of sight.

As they turned to look back up the hill, the massive white tip of a turning blade floated over the horizon. A second sail followed the first and then a third. Each one cut the air with a deep swoosh.

Jenny pulled her father in close and sheltered against the wind.

"The perfect gully, that's what Windy called it," said Pavel. "A natural wind tunnel."

Three giant windmills spun gracefully in the gully above Hushwish Bay, out of sight unless stumbled on by mistake. Windy had indeed found the perfect spot.

"So you allowed them to build the windmills to help the other farmers, then, Mr MacLeod?" asked Pavel.

Hamish steadied himself on his shepherd's crook for a moment before handing it to Pavel. "I hear your father taught you well, Pavel. Perhaps you'll help Jenny tend the sheep here after I'm gone. Look after this place and the people who are lucky enough to live here."

"You're not going anywhere, Dad," protested Jenny.

Hamish patted Jenny's hair and kissed the top of her head. "You see, we found a site for these things we could live with. The other crofters and farmers couldn't have lived here without them."

"You signed up so they could all keep farming here?" asked Pavel.

"Oh, I'm sure some of them could have managed. I did it for the next generation and the next one after that. They might find something else one day that doesn't make such a mark on the land, but, in moderation, I think these things are probably the best we can do for the moment."

Pavel checked his watch. "At this very moment, my mum and dad will be renewing their marriage vows," he said.

"In Mauritius," added Jenny. "I found it on the map, Dad. It's off the coast of Madagascar."

Her dad chuckled. "I bet the sand isn't as white or the sea as blue as it is here."

They all turned away from the windmills and looked down over Hushwish Bay.

"Never in a million years," said Jenny.

"Nice one," laughed Pavel.

"I didn't mean it," laughed Jenny. "I didn't mean to come out with one of your stupid sayings." She shoved him.

For a moment, Pavel wobbled on the heather before planting the shepherd's crook into the ground. He pulled himself up and laughed even harder.

Lord barked and wagged his tail.

"I'm glad you two made up," said her dad.

"Come on, Pavel," said Jenny. "I'll race you to the beach!"

"Wait!" said Pavel. "You got a head start."

"Better fast than last!" yelled Jenny.

Pavel stumbled forward. "Hey!"

The western wind was warm against Jenny's face as she ran. The tumbling waves filled her ears and the taste of summer filled her mouth.

She was home. She was home in her beautiful bay.

THE END